woodshop Storage Solutions

RALPH LAUGHTON

POPULAR WOODWORKING BOOKS
CINCINNATI, OHIO
www.popularwoodworking.com

read this important safety notice

To prevent accidents, keep safety in mind while you work. Use the safety guards installed on power equipment; they are for your protection. When working on power equipment, keep fingers away from saw blades, wear safety goggles to prevent injuries from flying wood chips and sawdust, wear hearing protection and consider installing a dust vacuum to reduce the amount of airborne sawdust in your woodshop. Don't wear loose clothing—such as neckties or loose-sleeved shirts, or jewelry—such as rings, necklaces or bracelets—when working on power equipment. Tie back long hair to prevent it from getting caught in your equipment. People who are sensitive to certain chemicals should check the chemical content of any product before using it. The authors and editors who compiled this book have tried to make the contents as accurate and correct as possible. Plans, illustrations, photographs and text have been carefully checked. All instructions, plans and projects should be carefully read, studied and understood before construction begins. Due to the variability of local conditions, construction materials, skill levels, etc., neither the author nor Popular Woodworking Books assumes any responsibility for any accidents, injuries, damages or other losses incurred resulting from the material presented in this book. Prices listed for supplies and equipment were current at the time of publication and are subject to change. Glass shelving should have all edges polished and must be tempered. Untempered glass shelves may shatter and can cause serious bodily injury. Tempered shelves are very strong and if they break will just crumble, minimizing personal injury.

metric conversion chart

to convert	to	multiply by
Inches	Centimeters	2.54
Centimeters	Inches	0.4
Feet	Centimeters	30.5
Centimeters	Feet	0.03
Yards	Meters	0.9
Meters	Yards	1.1

Distributed in Canada by Fraser Direct
100 Armstrong Avenue
Georgetown, Ontario L7G 5S4
Canada

Distributed in the U.K. and Europe by David & Charles
Brunel House
Newton Abbot
Devon TQ12 4PU
England
Tel: 01626 323200   Fax: 01626 323319
E-mail: postmaster@davidandcharles.co.uk

Distributed in Australia by Capricorn Link
P.O. Box 704
Windsor, NSW 2756
Australia

Visit our Web site at www.popularwoodworking.com for information on more resources for woodworkers.

Other fine Popular Woodworking Books are available from your local bookstore or direct from the publisher.

10   09   08   07   06   5   4   3   2   1

Library of Congress Cataloging-in-Publication Data

Laughton, Ralph, 1956-
  Woodshop storage solutions / by Ralph Laughton. -- 1st ed.
    p. cm.
  Includes bibliographical references and index.
  ISBN-13: 978-155870-784-9 (pbk. : alk. paper)
  ISBN-10: 1-55870-784-0 (pbk. : alk. paper)

  ISBN -13: 978-1-55870-812-9 (hc. : alk paper)
  ISBN -10: 1-55870-812-X (hc. : alk paper)
1. Workshops--Equipment and supplies. 2. Workshops--Design and construction. 3. Storage cabinets--Design and construction. 4. Woodwork. I. Title.

TT152.L38 2006
684.1'6--dc22

2006016902

Acquisitions/Editor: Jim Stack
Cover Designer: Brian Roeth
Designer/Page Layout: Dragonfly Graphics, L.L.C.
Illustrator: Len Churchill
Photographer: Ralph Laughton
Production coordinator: Jennifer L. Wagner

dedication

In memory of
Danny Proulx
1947–2004

about the author

Ralph Laughton originally trained as an engineer but did not follow that path; instead, on leaving full-time education, he embarked on a career as an editor for a specialist publisher. This led him into the world of graphic design, where he found it possible to indulge a creative passion for well over 20 years. Then he decided to take a life-changing opportunity and make his lifelong passion a reality. Now a full-time woodworker, he is designing and building furniture, repairing old joinery and writing about the techniques he has spent nearly 40 years acquiring. He is an established author of woodworking books and a regular contributor to several U.K. woodworking magazines.

acknowledgements

I would like to thank the following people for their help in the compilation of this book:

First, I would like to pay tribute to the late Danny Proulx. Without his encouragement and help I would not be writing this book. He was a prolific and knowledgeable writer of the many and varied techniques involved in woodworking and will be sorely missed.

My thanks are due to the good people at Trend Machinery & Cutting Tools Ltd. for their support with routing and cutters, DeWALT UK, Screwfix Direct and all the other people too numerous to mention who have helped out over the years.

Most of all, thanks are due to my long-suffering wife, Sue, who has not only read each and every word but has actively helped with the work shown in this book and collaborated on the design and photography of its content. She did this, as well as feeding and watering a sometimes grumpy and tired husband.

contents

introduction page 6

PROJECT 1
chisel rack page 8

PROJECT 2
sandpaper press page 12

PROJECT 3
small-items chest page 18

PROJECT 4
router-cutters storage cabinet page 26

PROJECT 5
drill press cabinet page 36

PROJECT 6
tool tote and stool page 46

PROJECT 7
small offcuts storage trolley page 54

PROJECT 8
wall-hung cabinet page 62

PROJECT 9
downdraft table page 70

PROJECT 10
clamp stand page 78

PROJECT 11
mobile table saw stand page 84

PROJECT 12
outfeed table page 90

PROJECT 13
freestanding cabinet page 96

PROJECT 14
router trolley page 104

PROJECT 15
computer station page 112

PROJECT 16
router table page 118

suppliers page 126
index page 127

This book is the story of a journey of discovery

made over several years. It shows that no matter how large or small a workshop there is always something that can be made to improve the workshop's usefulness. The projects here are real: all have been built to solve a particular problem and are in use today.

The three locations where the projects have been built cover the whole spectrum of size and available equipment. The largest workshop was a small commercial unit covering 1250 square feet (116 square meters) with high ceilings and level access through roller shutters to a road-accessible yard. Some of the larger projects as well as some smaller things were built there.

The smallest venue for sawdust making is my 8' × 6' (244cm × 183cm) garden shed. This was the main workshop for the house, and all sorts of projects have been produced there over the 20-plus years it has been in use—everything from reproduction windows for our Victorian house to the small, simple, invaluable chisel stand.

The final venue is our new modestly sized home workshop, which has been built over the past couple of years. This is a purpose-made wooden building with an internal dimension of 18' × 12' (549cm × 366cm).

So you can see that whatever the size of your workshop or however limited your selection of tools, you can find something here for you.

chisel rack

Now to make something . . .

The projects in this book are all useful. Some will take a lot of work and result in substantial pieces of floor-standing furniture. Others will be just as useful but entail very little work. To get the ball rolling, here is one of the most simple little projects you are likely to encounter; nevertheless, it'll be a most useful addition to a shop.

Chisels are best kept close at hand and in a manner that enables the user to select the correct size of chisel for the job as opposed to the first one that can be found. Of course, I would never compromise and use the only chisel I could lay my hand on . . . no, no, not me.

A rack is the best option, but it should not be a fixed rack, screwed to the wall. A sort of desk tidy for the bench that can be conveniently positioned for the job at hand is the idea here. As all the handles are similar, the only way to know which chisel is being selected is to be able to see the blade. Standing the chisels with the blades up in a container would solve that problem but create another! A more sensible solution is to suspend them in a rack that has a solid back and has a piece of wood fixed across the lower portion of the front. This will make the sizes of the blades visible but prevent the sharp ends from harming anything else—like me.

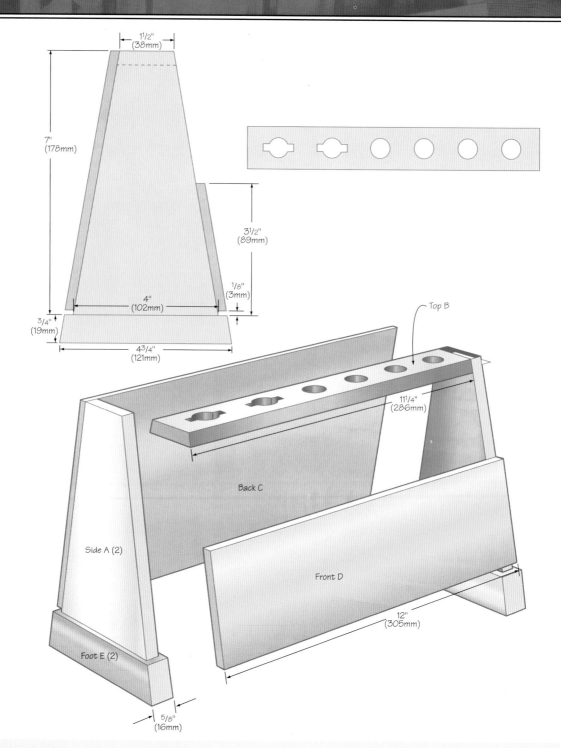

chisel rack inches (millimeters)

REFERENCE	QUANTITY	PART	STOCK	THICKNESS		WIDTH		LENGTH		COMMENTS
A	2	legs	MDF	3/8	(10)	4	(102)	7	(178)	
B	1	top	hardwood	3/8	(10)	1 1/2	(38)	11 1/4	(286)	
C	1	back	MDF	1/4	(6)	7	(178)	12	(305)	
D	1	front	MDF	1/4	(6)	3 1/2	(89)	12	(305)	
E	2	feet	hardwood	5/8	(16)	3/4	(19)	4 3/4	(121)	

1 The holes in the top of the rack can be made using a drill or a Forstner bit. However a cleaner hole can be easily cut using a small router and a template. This technique will enable any size of hole to be made without the need to buy lots of large drill bits that you may only use once. Although overkill used here, the method is worth illustrating. Any large hole cutter or Forstner bit can be used to make the template; use the appropriate bushing-guided cutter to cut the required-size hole.

2 Make a template with an appropriate hole cut in it, in this case one with a 1¼" (32mm) diameter, and mark the quadrants. Add to the template a fence that is ⅛" (3mm) from the edge of the hole. Cut a strip of wood 1½" (38mm) wide and 12" (305mm) long. Mark it up with a center line along its length and six cross lines at 2" (51mm) centers starting 1" (25mm) in from the end.

3 Align the hole-cutting jig with the cross lines and cut the six holes; the fence will ensure that all the holes are perfectly aligned. The fence will center the jig, and all that you need to do is align the cross lines to ensure even spacing. Clamp the template to the strip of wood or hold it in the vise using the fence to secure it. Use the router set up with an ¹¹⁄₁₆"-diameter (17mm) guide bushing and a ¼" (6mm) cutter.

4 Slot the two end holes using the ¼" (6mm) cutter so that they accept the two larger chisels.

5 Cut the ends from ⅜" (9mm) MDF and make them wider at the bottom than the top to aid stability. Chamfer or angle the top to match the sides. Add the back as a solid piece mounted just a few millimeters short of the bottom of the legs. This will prevent the rack from rocking on an uneven surface. Add the front from about the halfway mark down to the same distance from the bottom as the back. Secure all the parts together using fine panel pins (small nails) and glue, and that's it. This very simple little project will prove itself to be one of the most useful things you ever make for the bench top, and it can be stored full of chisels on a shelf when not on active duty.

sandpaper press

You know how some

things can be irritating: the dog next door still barking at the cat five minutes after the cat has gone to sleep on today's newspaper, or the mobile phone going off just when you are trying listen to the latest baseball (or cricket) score. Well, the one thing that really grates on me is curly sandpaper—a change in humidity and off it goes trying to turn into sanding tubes.

The temporary solution has been the "scrap of plywood and a brick" approach. However, the time has come for a more professional solution to the problem. While we are in the mood for improvement we should make a simple cutting jig too.

The box needs to be just larger than a full sheet of sandpaper. Inside the box you'll use dividers between the sandpaper grades and a

weight to keep the whole stack flat.

A full sheet of sandpaper measures 9" × 11" (230 × 280mm). The box interior needs to be slightly larger than that to allow the sheets to be inserted and removed without binding on the sides. The dividers are 1/16" (2mm) less than the width of the box interior and the same length. They get profile cuts to make tabs that can be labelled on the front edge.

The carcass of the box gets made from 3/4" (18mm) medium-density fiberboard (MDF), painted gray and edged with walnut. The 1/4" (6mm) MDF back is set with a loose fit into grooves in the carcass. The weight gets made from a sandwich of MDF and some sheet lead (roofing lead offcut).

A simple sandpaper cutting jig and sized templates get built and stored on the top of the box.

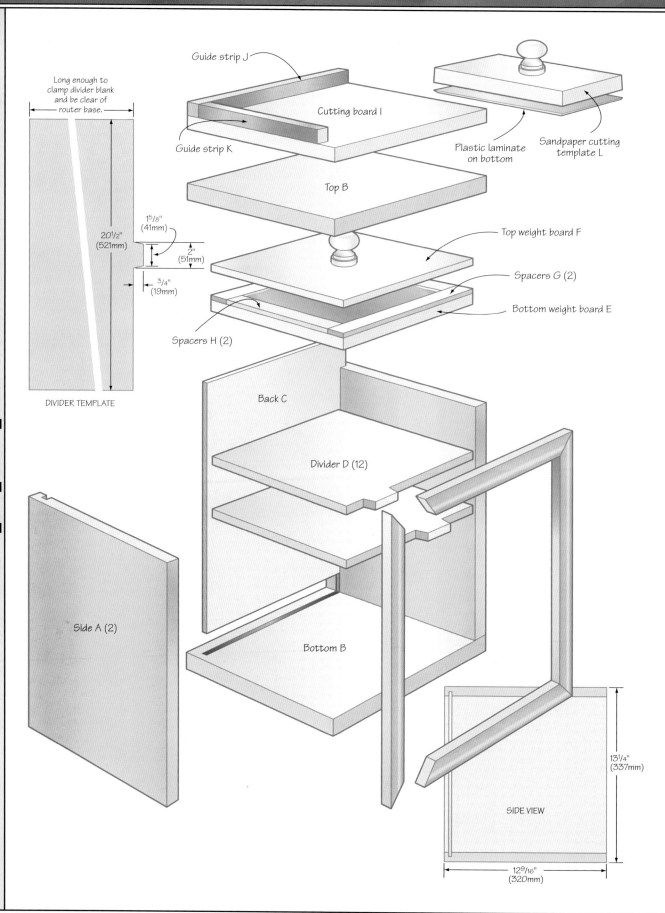

Guide strip J

Cutting board I

Guide strip K

Sandpaper cutting template L

Plastic laminate on bottom

Top B

Top weight board F

Long enough to clamp divider blank and be clear of router base.

20½" (521mm)

1⅝" (41mm)

2" (51mm)

¾" (19mm)

Spacers G (2)

Bottom weight board E

Spacers H (2)

DIVIDER TEMPLATE

Back C

Divider D (12)

Side A (2)

Bottom B

13¼" (337mm)

SIDE VIEW

12⁹⁄₁₆" (320mm)

sandpaper press inches (millimeters)

REFERENCE	QUANTITY	PART	STOCK	THICKNESS		WIDTH		LENGTH		COMMENTS
A	2	sides	MDF	$3/4$	(18)	$12^9/_{16}$	(320)	$11^3/_4$ h	(298)	
B	2	top and bottom	MDF	$3/4$	(18)	$10^5/_8$	(270)	$12^9/_{16}$	(320)	
C	1	back	MDF	$1/4$	(6)	$10^1/_8$	(257)	$12^3/_4$	(324)	
D	12	dividers	plywood	$1/4$	(6)	$9^1/_{16}$	(230)	$11^{13}/_{16}$	(300)	
E	1	bottom weight board	MDF	$3/4$	(18)	$9^1/_{16}$	(230)	$11^{13}/_{16}$	(300)	
F	1	top weight board	MDF	$1/4$	(6)	$9^1/_{16}$	(230)	$11^{13}/_{16}$	(300)	
G	2	spacers	MDF	$1/4$	(6)	$3/4$	(19)	$11^{13}/_{16}$	(300)	
H	2	spacers	MDF	$1/4$	(6)	$3/4$	(19)	$10^5/_{16}$	(262)	
I	1	cutting board	MDF	$3/4$	(18)	$10^5/_8$	(270)	$12^9/_{16}$	(320)	
J	1	guide strip	hardwood	$3/4$	(18)	$3/4$	(19)	$12^9/_{16}$	(320)	
K	1	guide strip	hardwood	$3/4$	(18)	$3/4$	(19)	$9^7/_8$	(251)	
L	1	sandpaper-cutting template	MDF	$3/4$	(18)	$4^1/_2$	(114)	$5^1/_2$	(140)	bottom is laminated, cut slight bevel on edges
M	1	sandpaper-cutting template	MDF	$3/4$	(18)	$4^1/_2$	(114)	11	(279)	bottom is laminated, cut slight bevel on edges

hardware & supplies

3 $1^1/_4$" (30mm)-diameter wooden knobs

roofing lead or other heavy material to use as weight

$1/4$" (6mm) x $3/4$" (18mm) x 50" (127cm) hardwood edging

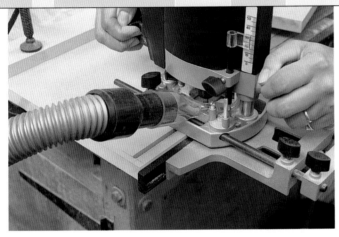

1 Rout the grooves in the carcass sides using a ¼"-diameter (6mm) straight cutter and a parallel guide fence attached to the router base.

2 Cut the biscuit slots using a simple right-angle jig. Rout the grooves for the back. Then dry assemble the parts to check for fit.

3 When all is ready, apply glue to the parts and clamp the assembly together. Make sure the box is square.

4 If you want to paint the box, do it now, before you apply the wood trim.

20MM TAB TEMPLATE.

5 Measure and fit the hardwood trim to the front face of the box.

6 Cut the dividers from thin plywood to the depth of the box and $3/32$" (2mm) narrower than the interior width. Next, make a template from a suitable piece of MDF to the dimensions shown in the drawing. This will be used to form the tabs on the front edge of the dividers. The tabs are cut so that four dividers can span the width of the box before the next one's tab position coincides with the first. The same template is used to cut all tabs by moving its position along the various dividers in increments of $2\frac{1}{4}$" (57mm).

7 Draw around the tab with a pencil. Remove the bulk of the waste with a jigsaw. Clamp the template in position with the template below the divider. Fit a small router—or as shown here, a laminate trimmer—with a bearing-guided flush-trim cutter. Trim the divider to the line. Reposition the template on the next divider, one tab position over, and repeat. Continue until you have enough dividers for your needs. It is a good idea to make a few extras at this time to cater to any future expansion of the sandpaper stock.

8 In order to keep the sandpaper flat, a weight is required. No, not that old brick—it does not match the color scheme! Cut one piece of $1/2$" (12mm) and one piece of $1/4$" (6mm) MDF to the same size as a full sheet of sandpaper, 9" × 11" (229 × 279mm). Cut some strips of $1/4$" (6mm) MDF to trim around the top surface of the $1/2$" (12mm) piece to make a tray. Cut a small square of the $1/4$" (6mm) MDF and glue it on the inside center of the board. This will act as a spacer and stop the sandwich compressing when the knob is fitted.

9 The other piece of MDF will make the top of the weight. Fill the void with something heavier than the MDF—an offcut of roofing lead is ideal. Alternatively, a steel plate could be used if you have the means to trim it to size. Sand could also be used, but make sure it is absolutely dry first.

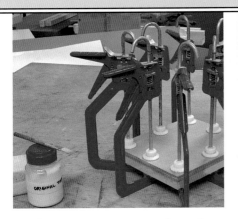

10 Glue the sandwich together and clamp. Let the glue cure overnight.

11 Drill a hole through the center and attach a wooden knob.

12 Cut a piece of $3/4$" (18mm) MDF to the same size as the top of the box. Trim the back and left-hand edge (right-hand edge if you are left-handed) with some strips of hardwood $3/4$" (18mm) square, to make an L-shaped alignment fence. Cut a second piece of MDF, this time from a $1/4$" (6mm) sheet, and $3/4$" (18mm) shorter and narrower than the first piece. This will act as a cutting board and can be replaced as it becomes worn.

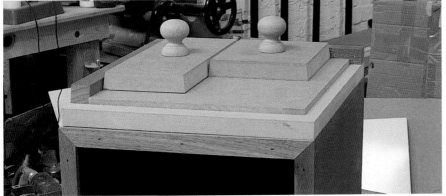

13 Cut the sandpaper templates from $3/4$" (18mm) MDF (which has been plastic laminated on the underside) at a slight angle on the edges in order to make cutting easier. This will provide a cleaner edge for the knife to follow. Make the templates to suit the sanders you have or the preferred size for hand sanding. Fix a wooden knob to the top surface, and the templates are ready to use.

14 To use the sandpaper cutter and templates, place a sheet of sandpaper facedown on the jig, pushed into the corner and against both fences. Select the required template and place it onto the back of the sandpaper also against both fences. Trim the paper along the edge of the template with a knife. It is possible to tear the finer grades along the edge of the template if you wish. When cutting smaller sheets it is advisable to cut the finished size from a precut sheet, e.g., cut quarter sheets from a precut half sheet. This will keep you from ending up with lots of L-shaped sheets.

15 Fill the sandpaper press with the coarse grade at the bottom, using the dividers to separate the various grades, and place the weight on top of the stack. No more curly sandpaper!

small-items chest

Well, I am amazed.

For years I have spent a great deal of my leisure time trying to enhance the productivity of my woodworking by improving my working conditions and automating my tool collection with the acquisition of power tools and machines. The trouble is that it is far too easy to start compromising the design to fit the tools, for example, letting the size that the jig will allow dictate the size of a dovetail.

Over the past couple of years I have spent some of the most enjoyable days of woodworking here in the garden shed getting back to

basics and hand tools. A nice new router is a great tool and it does a wonderful job, but nothing compares to enjoying the peace and quiet of the shed on a sunny afternoon while removing wafer-thin shavings of oak with a hand plane.

So why am I amazed? Because I am enjoying working with limited resources again. Nothing in this shed cost a fortune. The tools, although not the very cheapest, are all readily available at a local home improvement store or by mail order. The space, or lack of it, makes for creative solutions. And I am creating something — not just running a noisy tool to produce it.

small-items chest construction notes

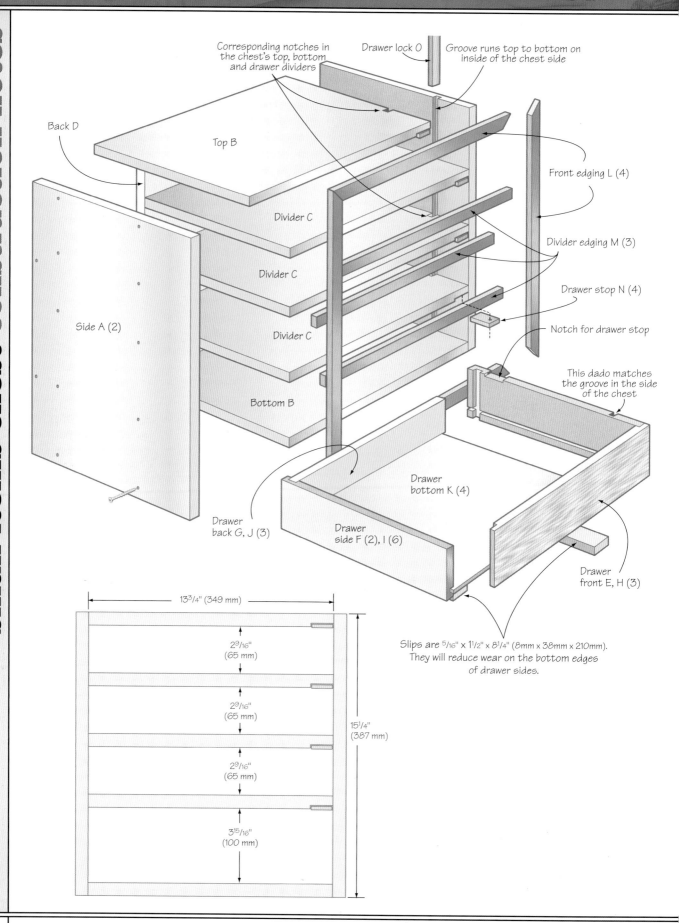

Corresponding notches in the chest's top, bottom and drawer dividers

Drawer lock O

Groove runs top to bottom on inside of the chest side

Back D

Top B

Front edging L (4)

Divider C

Divider C

Divider edging M (3)

Drawer stop N (4)

Divider C

Notch for drawer stop

Side A (2)

Bottom B

This dado matches the groove in the side of the chest

Drawer bottom K (4)

Drawer back G, J (3)

Drawer side F (2), I (6)

Drawer front E, H (3)

Slips are ⁵/₁₆" x 1¹/₂" x 8¹/₄" (8mm x 38mm x 210mm). They will reduce wear on the bottom edges of drawer sides.

13³/₄" (349 mm)

2⁹/₁₆" (65 mm)

2⁹/₁₆" (65 mm)

15¹/₄" (387 mm)

2⁹/₁₆" (65 mm)

3¹⁵/₁₆" (100 mm)

small-items chest inches (millimeters)

REFERENCE	QUANTITY	PART	STOCK	THICKNESS		WIDTH		LENGTH		COMMENTS
A	2	sides	MDF	3/4	(18)	10 d	(254)	15 1/4 h	(387)	
B	2	top and bottom	MDF	3/4	(18)	10 d	(254)	13 3/4	(350)	
C	3	dividers	MDF	3/4	(18)	9 1/4	(235)	13 3/4	(350)	
D	1	back	MDF	3/4	(18)	13 3/4	(350)	13 3/4	(350)	
E	1	drawer front	oak	3/4	(18)	3 15/16	(100)	13 3/4	(350)	
F	2	drawer sides	oak	1/2	(13)	3 7/8	(98)	9	(229)	
G	1	drawer back	oak	1/2	(13)	3 3/8	(86)	13 1/4	(337)	
H	3	drawer fronts	oak	3/4	(18)	2 9/16	(65)	13 3/4	(350)	
I	6	drawer sides	oak	1/2	(13)	2 1/2	(64)	9	(229)	
J	3	drawer backs	oak	1/2	(13)	2	(51)	13 1/4	(337)	
K	4	drawer bottoms	plywood	1/4	(6)	8 1/2	(216)	13 1/4	(337)	
L	4	front edgings	oak	1/4	(6)	3/4	(18)	15 1/4	(387)	
M	3	divider edgings	oak	1/4	(6)	3/4	(18)	13 3/4	(350)	
N	4	drawer stops	oak	1/4	(6)	1	(25)	2	(51)	
O	1	drawer lock	hardwood	1/4	(6)	1/2	(13)	15 1/4	(387)	

hardware & supplies

4 3"(75mm) homemade wooden drawer pulls

7 5/8" x 3/4" (194mm x 19mm) lay-flat chest handle

30 2"(50mm) carcass screws

4 3/4"(20mm) screws

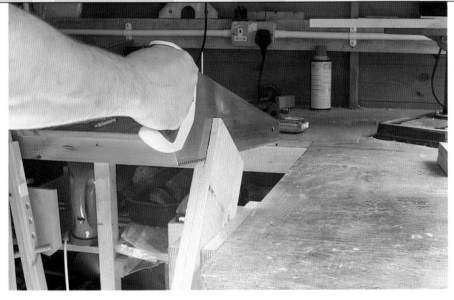

1 In a workshop full of tools, drawers can be knocked out with speed and precision. Saws and routers wailing away and the air thick with sawdust, the pile of soulless drawers grows rapidly. On the other hand, doing this by hand in the shed makes for an altogether relaxed affair. Design becomes what it should be: aesthetic and not primarily production efficient. Proportions can be dictated by function, and an awareness of the overall feel becomes paramount.

2 Planing one side of the oak flat. Plane the other side to thickness.

3 The kit of parts is labeled and ready for assembly.

4 Recess the drawer latches into the bottom of the drawer dividers and top using a guide bushing fitted to the router.

5 Cut the ¼" (6mm) × 1" (25mm) × 2" (51mm) recesses for the drawer stops using a router with a straight-cutting bearing-guided bit and a template cut from scrap material.

6 Attach the drawer stops using small screws. These stops are small pieces of wood that sit in the top of the drawer openings. The screw is tightened just enough to allow the latches to move. They will hang down at a slight angle after the chest is assembled. The drawer boxes have notches cut into them at the back of the right-hand sides. As the drawer is pulled forward, the latch will drop into the notch to stop the drawer. If the drawer is to be removed, the latch can be lifted with your finger while pulling out the drawer.

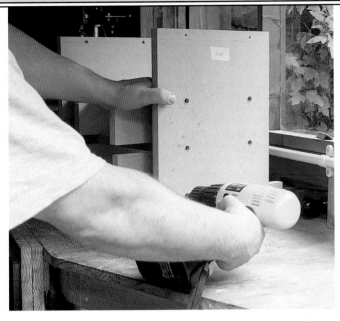

7 Pilot and counterbore the sides and dividers. Using drywall screws, assemble the drawer box.

8 Then plug the counterbored screw holes with wooden plugs.

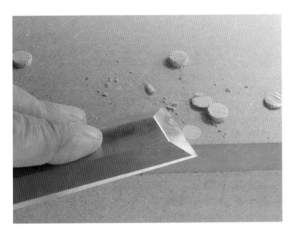

9 Trim the wooden plugs flush to the surface of the drawer box using a sharp chisel. Cut and fit facing strips of oak. Using glue, attach them to the front edges of the drawer box.

10 Fit the drawer fronts to the openings in the drawer box. Note the notches with the drawer stops installed. After the hardwood edging is attached, these will be invisible.

11 Cut the drawer faces to rough length.

12 Final fit the drawer fronts using your handplane.

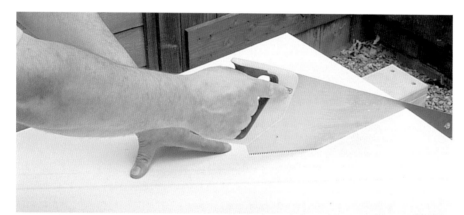

13 Cutting large sheets of material is easily handled using a handsaw. Here, I'm cutting the drawer bottoms to size.

14 The drawer faces are rebated (rabbetted) to accept the sides, and grooved to accept the bottoms. Two holes are drilled for the drawer pulls. The sides are cut to be the same height as the fronts and a groove is cut along their length to accept the bottom. A vertical housing is cut on the outside of the right-hand drawer side perfectly in line with the groove made in the cabinet side and a notch in the top. Two strips of oak are glued and pinned to the inside of the drawer sides below these grooves. These will help support the bottom and reduce the wear on the drawer dividers. The drawers are glued and pinned together. Then, the bottoms are installed and pinned in place through the bottom panel and into the bottom of the back.

15 The top three drawers are all the same size and the bottom drawer is made deeper in order to accommodate some larger items. But design this box to fit your own tools and needs.

16 The finished chest showing the handle attached to the top. Note the hole in the top that will accept the drawer lock that runs top to bottom inside the chest to lock the drawers when the chest is being transported.

17 The drawers are the perfect size for holding plastic compartments that can serve as dividers to separate smaller parts.

router-cutters
storage cabinet

The first

router I bought came with one cutter. It was a 1/4" (6mm), High-speed steel (HSS), single-flute straight cutter that burnt the wood and became dull after a few minutes of abuse in my inexperienced hands. I then found a manufacturer's catalog and discovered a whole new world of tungsten carbide (TC) router cutters: I thought I would never be able to afford them if they only lasted a few minutes! That was over 30 years ago, and my collection of router bits has since grown somewhat—I discovered how to not abuse them, of course!

Over the years I've aquired a large collection of cutters. The result is a box full of cutters I need to search through every time a particular cutter is required; picture a child raking through a box full of LEGO's searching for that elusive brick.

I wanted to organize the larger cutters by profile regardless of shank diameter. I also wanted to be able to identify each cutter with its own label. To make the best use of the space, one

shelf has two rows of holes that will accept 1/4" (6mm)-shank cutters. However, my collection of larger cutters is mounted on various-size shanks [5/16" (8mm), 3/8" (10mm) and 1/2" (13mm)]. The single most important thing has to be the ability to rearrange the positions of these cutters as the collection grows. This problem is resolved by using a standard size hole in the shelf that holds them and bushing the hole with a loose insert that matches the diameter of the shank. By moving the inserts around, you can house any cutter in any position. The shelf has a wide, shallow dovetail slot cut along the length of the front edge. Identification tags get sprung into position rather like the price labels on supermarket shelves. The cabinet is consructed from walnut with maple for the raised panel in the door and the back. The inserts get cut from a length of 25mm hardwood dowel. The cabinet gets assembled using dovetail joinery.

Enough is enough; it's time to build the cabinet!

router-cutters storage cabinet construction notes

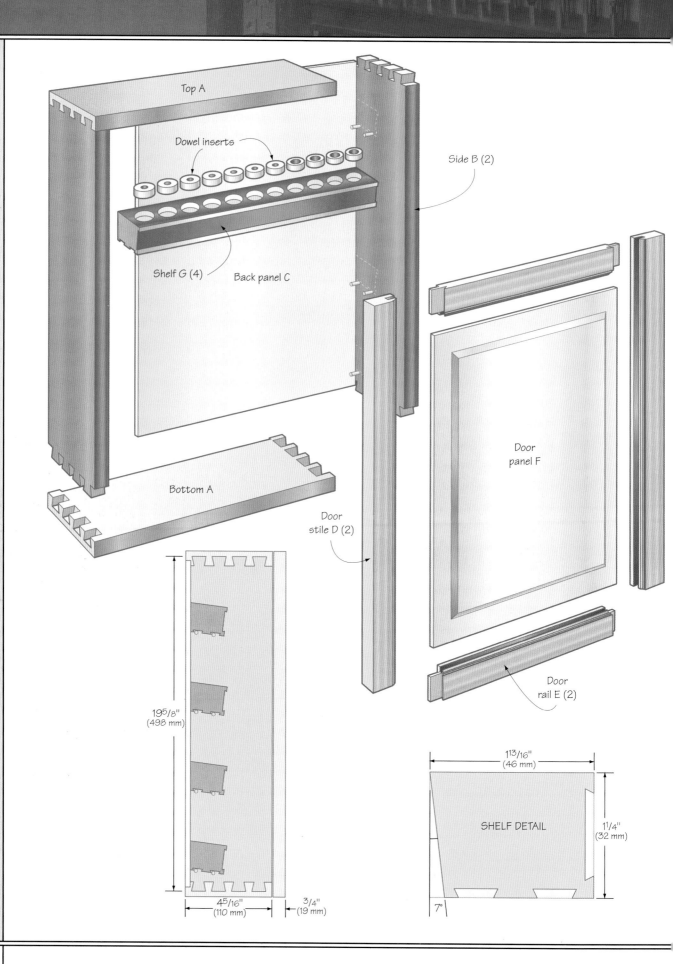

Top A

Dowel inserts

Side B (2)

Shelf G (4)   Back panel C

Bottom A

Door panel F

Door stile D (2)

Door rail E (2)

19⁵/₈"
(498 mm)

4⁵/₁₆"
(110 mm)

3/4"
(19 mm)

1¹³/₁₆"
(46 mm)

SHELF DETAIL

1¹/₄"
(32 mm)

7°

router-cutters storage cabinet inches (millimeters)

REFERENCE	QUANTITY	PART	STOCK	THICKNESS		WIDTH		LENGTH		COMMENTS
A	2	top and bottom	walnut	$3/4$	(19)	$4^{5}/16$	(110)	15	(381)	
B	2	sides	walnut	$3/4$	(19)	$4^{5}/16$	(110)	$19^{5}/8$	(498)	
C	1	back panel	maple	$1/4$	(6)	$14^{9}/16$	(370)	$19^{5}/16$	(490)	
D	2	door stiles	walnut	$3/4$	(19)	2	(51)	$20^{1}/4$	(521)	
E	2	door rails	walnut	$3/4$	(19)	2	(51)	12	(305)	
F	1	door panel	maple	$5/8$	(16)	$11^{1}/2$	(292)	$15^{3}/4$	(400)	
G	4	shelves	walnut	$1^{1}/4$	(32)	$1^{13}/16$	(46)	$13^{3}/8$	(340)	

hardware & supplies

2 $2^{1}/2$" (65mm) brass hinges

1 $1^{1}/4$"-diameter (30mm) wooden knob

16 65mm shelf pins

55 $1/2$" × 1"-diameter (13mm × 25mm) dowel inserts (number of inserts to be determined by your personal needs.)

1 A trip to the local lumber merchants resulted in a few lengths of hardwood of dubious character. The odd knot here and there and a waney edge or two makes a big difference in price. There is plenty of room to select knot-free wood from the clear areas.

2 To achieve a square finish from sawn boards it is important to start by planing a true, flat surface on one side of the boards. Look at the boards end on and determine whether there is any cupping in any of the boards. Place the boards to be machined with the crowns uppermost and plane until they are perfectly flat. Now set the fence on the jointer 90° to the table and plane one edge of each board. You now have face sides and face edges perpendicular to each other. Plane the boards to final thickness, cut to proper width and you're ready to start building the cabinet.

3 Route the profile on the door frame components. Use featherboards to keep the stock in contact with the cutter and reduce the risk of kickback.

4 Reconfigure the cutter to scribe mode as detailed in the manufacturer's instructions. Follow these instructions and you won't go wrong.

6 Make a gauge for setting the height of the panel raiser.

5 Use a push block as a backer to support the rail and prevent any tear-out while routing the scribe.

7 Use the gauge to set the height of the panel raiser. This is a quick, easy and accurate way to set the cutter height.

8 The door panel blank is wider than the lumber, so glue up enough stock to make the proper width.

9 Use a planer to flatten and cut the door panel to the proper thickness.

10 Make the first pass of the door insert. When using a panel cutter, make partial cuts instead of hogging the entire cut in one pass.

11 For this panel, four small incremental cuts gets the panel raised properly. Note the clean cuts. Making small cuts lets the cutter do its work without overworking, which can quickly dull the cutter and most likely leave burn marks in the wood.

adjusting dovetails

The cabinet is four pieces of walnut stock, dovetailed together with a thin maple back rebated (rabbeted) into it. Start by cutting the top and bottom to length. Using a dovetail jig and a router fitted with the ap-

propriate guide bushing and cutter, cut all the dovetails. Glue, clamp and check for square. When the assembly is dry, remove it from the clamps and rabbet the back edge to accept the maple back.

When cutting lap dovetails using a dovetail jig, the depth of the cutter will determine the tightness of the joint. Too deep and the joint will wobble; too shallow and the joint will be so tight you may not even be able to get the joint together. In soft woods, a little less tight can usually be accommodated by the inherent give in the wood. However, hardwoods such as walnut are far less forgiving. With a combination square as a depth gauge, the setting can be registered at the setup and checked between cuts to pick up any creep (from the original setting) that may have been caused by vibration during the cutting operation.

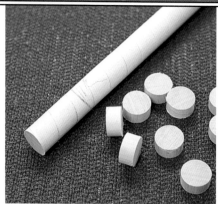

13 Cut some insert blanks from a hardwood dowel. Cut as many as you think you'll need, then cut about 10 more for future additions to your collection of cutters.

12 Check the fit of all the door parts prior to gluing.

14 Clamp the blanks in place and drill properly sized holes to accept the shanks of your router cutters.

15 Use a Forstner bit and guide fence on the drill press to bore the 1" (25mm) sockets in the shelves.

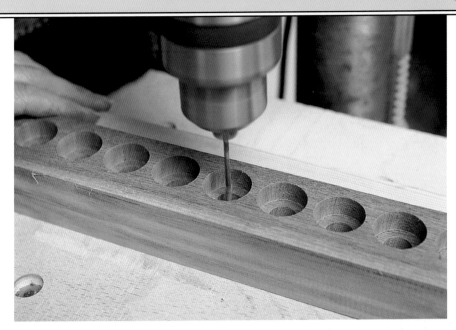

16 Drill the air holes with the fence kept in the same position as step 15.

17 Drill three shelves with sockets. (The bottom one shows a test hole in the waste area.) The top shelf is to be drilled for the smaller $1/4$" (6mm) shank cutters.

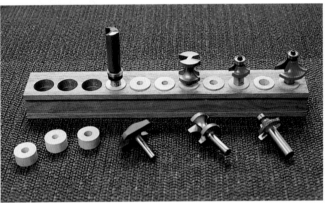

18 Test fit cutters in various-size inserts. This system of cutter storage allows you great freedom to organize.

19 Use a drilling template to properly locate the holes for the shelf supports. The template will ensure the correct positioning of holes on both sides.

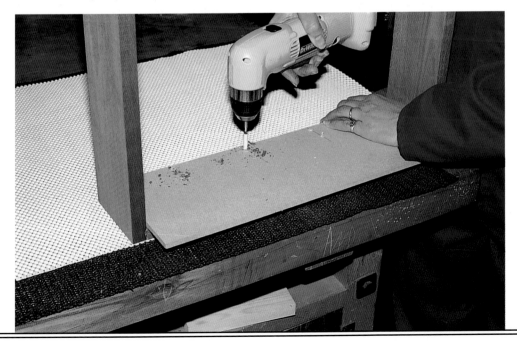

20 Use small panel pins or finish nails to secure the back of the cabinet in place.

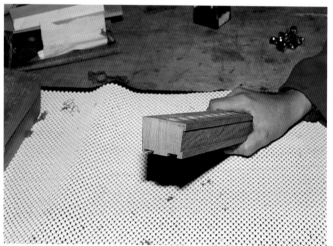

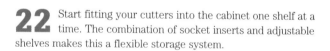

21 The end of a finished shelf shows the profile and shallow dovetail detail on the front edge. Note the two shallow grooves in the bottom of the shelf: These align with the shelf brackets to hold the shelf securely in place.

22 Start fitting your cutters into the cabinet one shelf at a time. The combination of socket inserts and adjustable shelves makes this a flexible storage system.

23 Install the hinges, attach the door and install the shelves.

24 Install a wooden knob and you're done. In addition to being functional, this cabinet is handsome!

hanging the cabinet

Use caution if you intend to hang the cabinet on the wall. Drilling through the back and screwing it to the wall will probably result in the back parting company from the carcass. Needless to say, neither the cutters nor the cabinet benefit from such a scenario! One way to avoid this

is to use mirror plates, intended as a means to secure mirrors (in frames) to walls or over fireplaces. Today, these small brass plates are frequently used to secure pictures to the walls in public places to prevent the pictures from being removed by the unscrupulous. In such situations, the plates are fitted so that the plate is visible and a screw can be inserted. However, by inverting them as shown in the photograph, you can secure them to the cabinet with screws through two of the holes and drill the back in line with the third hole. Now the cabinet can be hung on the wall with screws passing through the back and the plate.

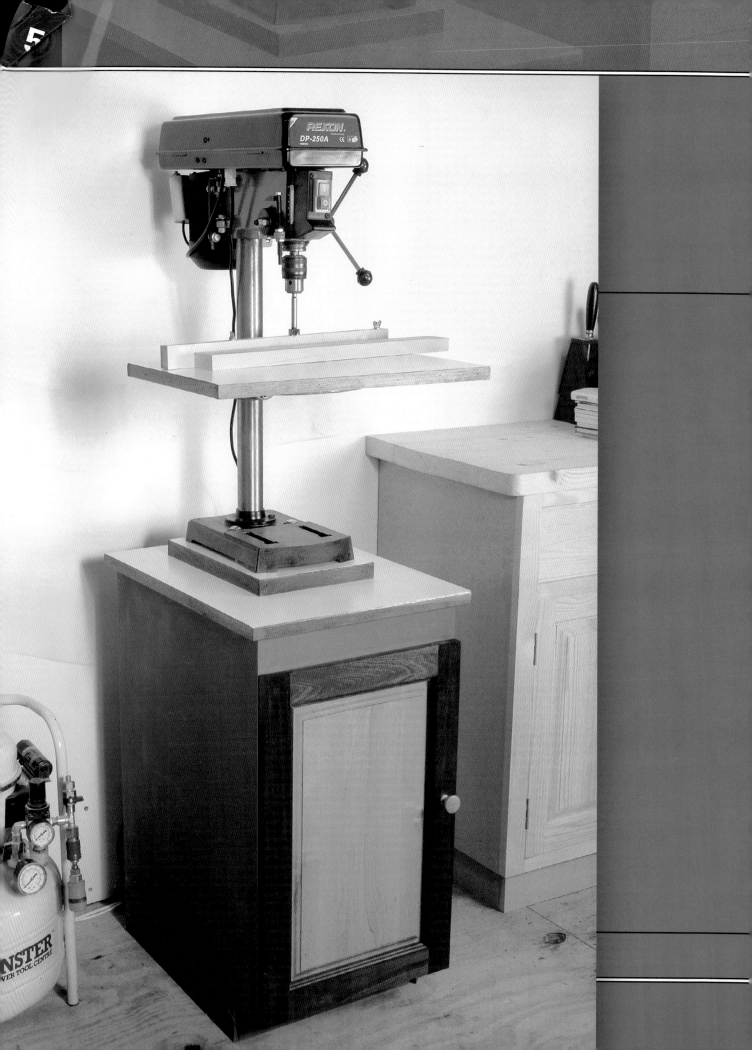

drill press cabinet

The small drill press is a

great little machine—so versatile yet underused if it has no permanent place to reside. For me this is due, in part, to my requirement to keep it portable so that I can use it outside of the workshop. If I need to sink a European hinge in a kitchen door, the drill press is portable enough to take in hand to the job. It spends most of its life hiding under benches in the workshop. I decided to give it the honor of its own dedicated space from where it could be used on a day-to-day basis or be ported out of the workshop to be put to work elsewhere.

The other thing it needs is a bespoke table or a worktop. An offcut of medium-density fiberboard (MDF) bolted to the table and a scrap of wood clamped in place for a fence works well in a temporary situation but needs to be much improved to be practical in its new come-and-use-me role!

The working height of the drill press is

something that only you can decide. The height I have opted for here is 31⅛" (791mm), which is the height of the folding bench it invariably came to rest on in the past. What suits me might not suit you, so you may modify the dimensions accordingly.

From an aesthetic point of view, the new piece of workshop furniture has to match the other cabinets in the grand workshop refit plan—OK, the other cabinet, but you have to start somewhere! This is made from solid walnut and maple, which is fine for a relatively small router cutter cabinet (project four) but could get a little expensive if used to build a floor-standing cabinet carcass. In order to keep the cost of this project reasonable, ¾"-thick (18mm) MDF is used to make a carcass for the walnut and maple door.

The new table is made from MDF edged with walnut and covered with plastic laminate. An adjustable fence is fabricated from maple to keep the theme going.

drill press cabinet construction notes

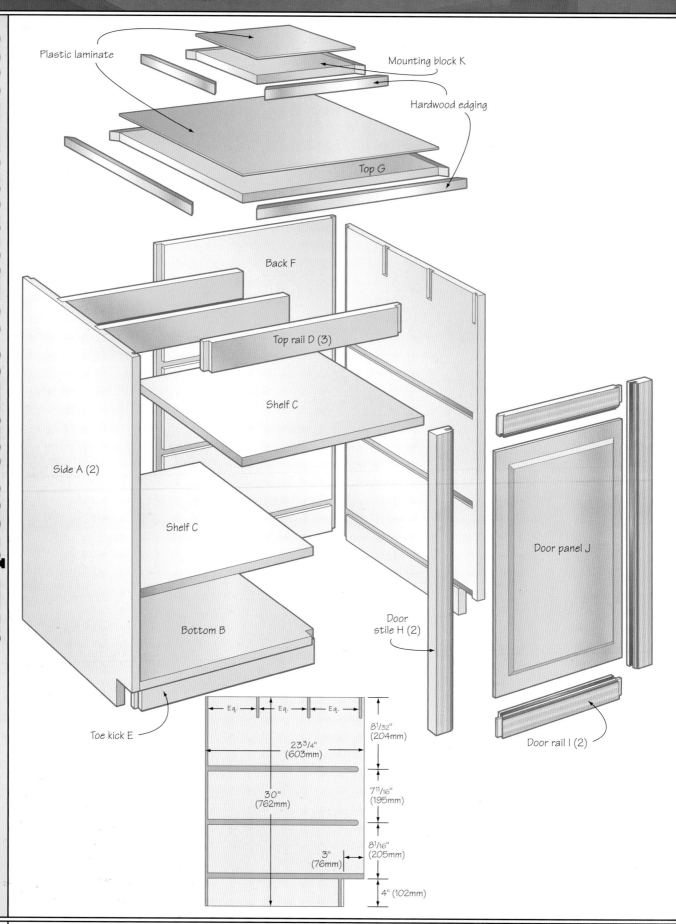

Plastic laminate

Mounting block K

Hardwood edging

Top G

Back F

Top rail D (3)

Shelf C

Side A (2)

Shelf C

Door panel J

Bottom B

Door stile H (2)

Toe kick E

Door rail I (2)

Eq.   Eq.   Eq.

8¹/32" (204mm)

23³/4" (603mm)

7¹¹/16" (195mm)

30" (762mm)

8¹/16" (205mm)

3" (76mm)

4" (102mm)

drill press cabinet inches (millimeters)

REFERENCE	QUANTITY	PART	STOCK	THICKNESS		WIDTH		LENGTH		COMMENTS
A	2	sides	MDF	3/4	(18)	23 3/4	(603)	30	(762)	
B	1	bottom	MDF	3/4	(18)	17 1/4	(438)	23 3/8	(594)	
C	2	shelves	MDF	3/4	(18)	17 1/4	(438)	22 3/8	(568)	
D	3	top rails	MDF	3/4	(18)	3	(76)	17 1/4	(438)	
E	1	toe kick	MDF	3/4	(18)	4	(102)	17 1/4	(438)	
F	1	back	MDF	3/4	(18)	17 1/4	(438)	30	(762)	
G	1	top	MDF	3/4	(18)	18 7/16	(468)	24 7/16	(621)	edged with hardwood
H	2	door stiles	hardwood	3/4	(18)	2 1/4	(57)	26	(660)	
I	2	door rails	hardwood	3/4	(18)	2 1/4	(57)	14 1/4	(362)	
J	1	door panel	hardwood	9/16	(14)	14	(356)	22	(559)	
K	1	mounting block	pine	1 1/8	(29)	10	(254)	10	(254)	edged with hardwood
	1	drill press table	MDF	3/4	(18)	12	(305)	24	(610)	edged with 3/4" (18) x 13/16" (21mm) hardwood, laminate
	1	drill press table fence	hardwood	1 1/8	(29)	2	(51)	24	(610)	

hardware & supplies

- 2   170° European hinges
- 1   1 1/4" (32mm)-diameter wooden knob
- 4   3/8 - 16 × 1 1/4" (10M x 1.5 x 30mm) carriage bolts
- 4   3/8" (10M) hex nuts
- 4   3/8" (10M) flat washers
- 4   3/8" (10M) lock washers
- 2   5/16 - 18 × 3" (8M x 1.25 x 75mm) carriage bolts
- 1   5/16" (8M) hex nut
- 1   5/16" (8M) wing nut
- 2   5/16" (8M) flat washers
-     7/16" × 3/4" × 250" (11mm × 18mm × 635cm) hardwood trim

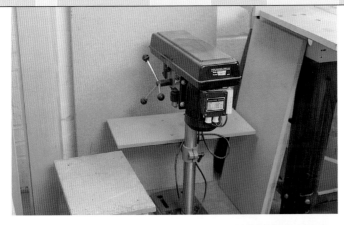

1 Drill press under bench—Ah! There it is...

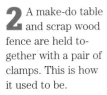

2 A make-do table and scrap wood fence are held together with a pair of clamps. This is how it used to be.

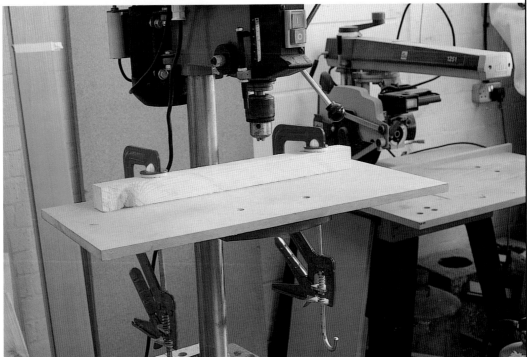

3 Cut out the parts for the cabinet. Trim the recess for the kick space in the side panels.

4 Lay the sides on a bench with their back edges touching and in perfect alignment. Mark the locations for the shelf and bottom panel housings (dadoes). Use a straightedge guide and a $^{23}/_{32}$"-diameter (18mm) straight cutter to rout the dadoes.

5 Cut the upper dadoes, for the dividers, back and the toe kick.

6 Add glue to the dadoes and assemble the cabinet.

7 Toenail the parts in place to add extra strength to the cabinet.

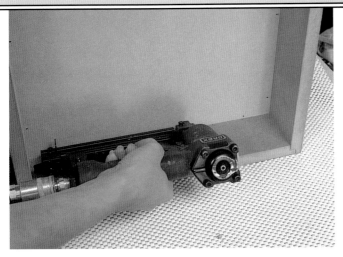

8 Select the maple pieces from which the door panel blank is to be made, and trim them to rough length. Be sure the mating edges are square and true. Place the boards together in their intended orientation and mark out the finished size and position of biscuits. Keep the biscuits within the raised area to avoid them showing after the panel has been routed. Then cut the biscuit slots.

9 Glue up the panel. Set it aside to let the glue cure.

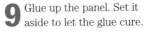

10 Rout the profile on the door rails and stiles.

11 Rout the end profile on each end of the rails. Use a backer board to prevent tear-out on the rails.

12 Rout the profile of the door panel. Make this cut in several light passes.

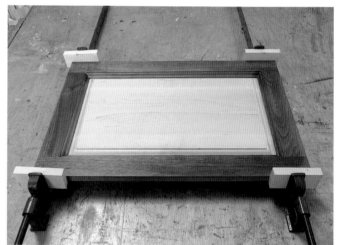

13 Assemble the door and check it for squareness.

14 Trim the worktop with walnut strips secured with No. 10 biscuits.

15 Pour some contact adhesive into a jar, and use a brush to apply a thin coat to the surface of the MDF and trim. Let this dry about 20 minutes, then apply a second coat. Finally, apply a coat to the back of the plastic laminate, and set this aside until almost dry—about 10 minutes. (If the humidity is high, it will take longer for the contact adhesive to dry.)

16 When the contact adhesive is dry to the touch, place thin strips of wood over the glued surface and position the laminate on top of them.

17 Remove the strips, starting in the center and working toward the outside. Apply pressure with the aid of a J-roller.

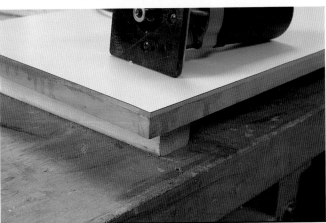

18 Use a trim router to cut the laminate flush with the edges of the top.

19 Use knockdown blocks to secure the top to the carcass.

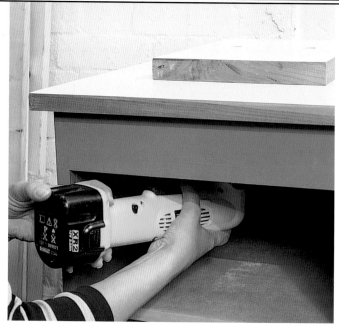

20 Make the mounting block from a $1\frac{1}{8}$"-thick (29mm) piece of pine edged with walnut and laminated and trimmed the same as the top. Drill two holes through it to align with the cast base of the drill press. Then position the block on the top of the cabinet and secure it from underneath with screws. Extend the two mounting holes through the top. Secure the drill press in position with bolts, nuts and washers.

21 Cut out the drill press table. Drill and counterbore four holes from the top of the table to coincide with the outer end of the slots on the drill press's metal table. Pass four bolts through the holes and hold them in place with an epoxy filler. When the filler is dry, sand the filler flush with the MDF. Edge the table with hardwood and laminate the top. Then mount the table on the metal table of the drill press and secure it with washers and hex nuts threaded onto the captured bolts.

22 Make a template from $\frac{1}{4}$"-thick (6mm) MDF for the sacrificial insert. The size of the insert should be about 3" (76mm) square. Using a guide bushing and collar, cut the recess to a depth of $\frac{1}{2}$" (12 mm). Square the corners with a sharp chisel, taking care not to chip the laminate.

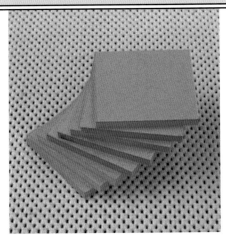

23 Remove the collar from the guide bushing and use the same template to cut squares from ½"-thick (12mm) MDF. These can be inserted into the recess and replaced when required.

24 Drill a small hole 1" (25mm) in from the back right-hand side of the table. Mount a single rod in a router fitted with a $^5/_{16}$"-diameter (8mm) straight cutter. Fit a trammel pivot onto the other end of the rod and cut an arc starting 1" (25mm) in from the back of the table to a point just forward of the center line of the drill's chuck.

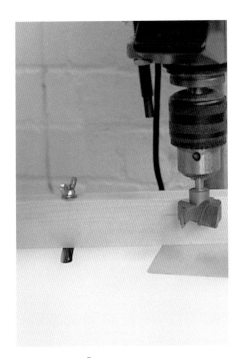

26 Using the new worktop and adjustable fence to hold the door in place, drill holes for the hinges. Install the hinges and hang the door.

25 Drill a $^5/_{16}$" (8mm)-diameter hole at one end of the fence to align with the hole in the table and a second hole at the other end to align with the arc. Use bolts, washers and wing nuts or threaded knobs to lock the fence into its required position.

tool tote & stool

If you have the luxury

of your own workshop you probably have all your tools stored in beautifully crafted cabinets. Each tool has its place and is judiciously replaced after each use, but not before it has been cleaned and lightly oiled. The cabinets were built with foresight so that no matter what new tools are acquired there will always be room for them. By the way, the skylight in the workshop is to observe the pigs as they fly by.

Reality dictates that no matter how good the intentions, more storage places are needed than are available. The ever increasing tool collection evolves into groups: bench tools, home repair tools, metalworking tools, etc. However some tools—hammers, screwdrivers, saws, measuring tools and so forth—are needed regardless of the job.

Rather than gathering these tools from storage in a fixed cabinet, you can use a tool

tote of some kind to house these frequently required tools. You can then take it to the workplace, whether that is at the bench, in the house or in the garden, for that matter. The problem I have found with this is that the tote or caddy needs somewhere to sit while you work. Parking it on the floor is inconvenient if you are working at the bench in the shop or on a portable bench elsewhere.

Building a stand for the caddy would solve the height problem but would hardly justify the effort. However if you were to build something useful that could also double as a stand, well that's a different matter.

A stool is the answer. It consists of a top surface that matches the dimensions of the toolbox, a pair of legs and a stretcher. The legs splay slightly wider than the width of the top and are splayed to match the length. A handhold cut into the top and clearance in the top of the stretcher allow for fingers to pass through, making it easy to move from one location to another.

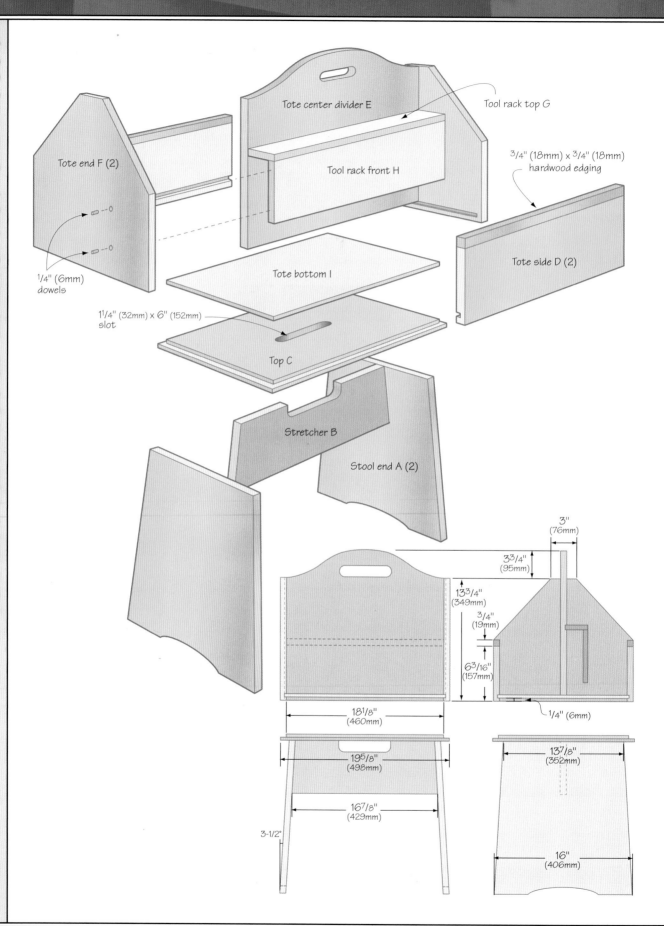

Tote center divider E

Tool rack top G

Tote end F (2)

Tool rack front H

$^3/_4$" (18mm) x $^3/_4$" (18mm) hardwood edging

$^1/_4$" (6mm) dowels

Tote side D (2)

Tote bottom I

$1^1/_4$" (32mm) x 6" (152mm) slot

Top C

Stretcher B

Stool end A (2)

3" (76mm)

$3^3/_4$" (95mm)

$13^3/_4$" (349mm)

$^3/_4$" (19mm)

$6^3/_16$" (157mm)

$^1/_4$" (6mm)

$18^1/_8$" (460mm)

$19^5/_8$" (498mm)

$16^7/_8$" (429mm)

$13^7/_8$" (352mm)

16" (406mm)

3-1/2°

tool tote & stool inches (millimeters)

REFERENCE	QUANTITY	PART	STOCK	THICKNESS		WIDTH		LENGTH		COMMENTS
A	2	stool ends	MDF	3/4	(18)	16	(406)	16	(406)	
B	1	stretcher	MDF	3/4	(18)	6	(152)	16^7/8	(429)	3^1/2° angle both ends
C	1	top	MDF	3/4	(18)	19^5/8	(498)	16^3/8	(416)	
D	2	tote sides	MDF	3/4	(18)	6^3/16	(157)	18^1/8	(460)	
E	1	tote center divider	MDF	3/4	(18)	17	(432)	18^5/8	(473)	
F	2	tote ends	MDF	3/4	(18)	16^1/8	(410)	13^3/4 h	(349)	
G	1	tool rack top	MDF	1/2	(12)	2^1/2	(64)	18^1/8	(460)	
H	1	tool rack front	MDF	1/2	(12)	6^5/8	(168)	18^1/8	(460)	
I	1	tote bottom	plywood	1/4	(6)	12^3/4	(324)	18^5/8	(473)	

1 The original stools are still in use years after they were consigned to the skip.

2 How many tools can you fit in a tool tote? The original tote is too big for domestic use and gets heavier on every outing.

3 Begin by building the tool tote. To protect the top edges of the sides, lip them with hardwood strips. You could use birch-faced cabinet-grade plywood instead of MDF, but that would be fairly expensive and, lets face it, this box is meant to be functional. Good looks are a bonus here. Use biscuits and glue to attach the strips to the sides. Then, use a router and a roundover bit to rout the inner edge of the hardwood lipping. Leave the outer edge square, and remove the arris with a single stroke of a finely set block plane.

4 Route a 1/4" (6mm) wide by 1/4" (6mm) deep groove along the bottom inside edge of the side (the same side as the roundover) to accept the plywood bottom.

5 Cut the stopped grooves for the bottom using the router setup used to cut the grooves in the sides. Then cut the ends to shape.

6 Cut a vertical groove in the end panels for the center divider. This groove can be cut with a 23/32"-diameter (18mm) straight cutter.

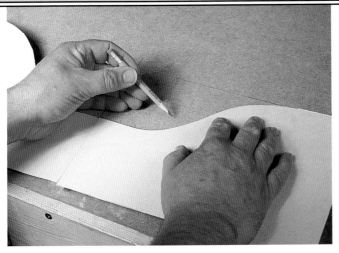

7 Use cardboard to make a template for the curve of the hand-hold. Fold the cardboard in half, draw half the profile, and cut it out. Unfold the template and you'll have a perfectly symmetrical pattern for the shape of the handhold. Use the template to mark the curve on the top of the divider.

8 Rough-cut the shape of the divider using a jigsaw.

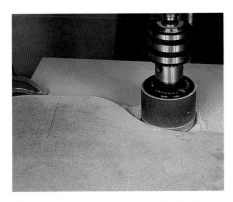

9 Sand to the line of the handhold shape. Here I'm using a 3"-diameter (76mm) sanding drum in the drill press. Cut the handhold using a 1¼" (32mm) spade bit. Bore the holes from each side to the center to avoid breaking out the MDF. Join the holes using a jigsaw, and sand smooth. Use a bearing-guided roundover cutter to smooth the edges of the cutout. Then cut a horizontal groove in the center divider for the tool rack.

10 Use biscuits and glue to join the sides to one end, and insert screws through the ends into the sides. Then set the plywood base into the groove and secure the other end in place using biscuits, glue and screws. Glue the central divider into the grooves in the sides and secure it with screws.

11 Toenail the bottom into the sides from underneath and screw it to the bottom edge of the divider to further strengthen the tote.

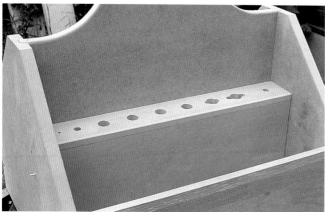

12 Make the chisel and tool rack from ½"-thick (12mm) MDF. Drill holes or make slots to accommodate the tools that you are going to store in it. Round over the front edge. Glue the rack into the groove cut into the divider.

13 Attach a front skirt to the tool rack to prevent the sharp edges of the chisels from getting damaged and causing damage (mainly to you!). Secure it in place using glue and small dowels driven through the ends of the tote.

14 Use spring clips to hold other tools in place. To hold the tape measure, you can make a strap from a section of hacksaw blade, with the teeth ground off, and install washers to act as spacers.

16 Move on to the stool. Cut the legs to of the stool to size and shape. Lay out the curve at the bottom. Make the cutout to create feet, which prevent the stool from rocking on an uneven surface. Cut the stretcher to size, and cut out the space for the handhold. Attach the two legs to the stretcher using glue and screws. Then plug the screw holes and trim the plugs flush to the surface of the legs. Cut the top to size and attach it to the leg assembly using glue and screws.

15 Trim the dowels flush to the sides and sand the tote smooth. Seal the MDF with a coat or two of sanding sealer and a clear varnish. The tool tote is ready to be filled with your cherished tools and pressed into service.

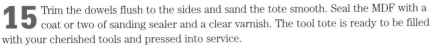

17 Using a straight cutter and a parallel fence attached to a router base, cut a rabbet $1/4$" (6mm) deep by $23/32$" (18mm) wide around the top surface. Cut the handhold using a $1^1/4$" (32mm) spade bit. Join the holes using a jigsaw and sand smooth. Use a bearing-guided roundover cutter to smooth the edges of the cutout. Check that the tool tote fits onto the rabbet and adjust the rabbet if necessary.

18 Seal the MDF of the stool with a coat or two of sanding sealer and a clear varnish. The stool can be used as a sawhorse or as a stool.

small offcuts
storage trolley

There comes a point when

the offcuts that might come in handy one day become a liability, a stack in the corner that is constantly falling over or getting in the way. Next comes a great temptation to clear it all out and start again. After all, finding a suitable piece of wood in that chaos becomes harder and harder. The thought of going through all those pieces of wood, expecting a cascade of wood every time the stack slips a little, is just too much. I am sure you know the feeling.

I have tried the "chuck it if it is under a certain length or width" routine and have even done some major clearing out from time to time, but the pile still becomes unmanageable very quickly. The trouble is that as soon as that piece of oak strip gets thrown out, a use for it arises the very next day.

What this lot needs is a home: not a big home, but a relatively small home that can be

moved around easily to a convenient position when it is needed and out of the way when it is not.

This unit is not for storing large pieces or even sheet goods—these are all stored elsewhere and do not create the same problems. This is for all those small strips, dowel lengths and blocks. The whole thing is only 19⅝" (498mm) wide and 14" (356mm) deep. The small size will automatically limit your collection—if a piece will not fit because the compartment is full, either swap it or get rid of it.

This restriction will pare your collection down to useful pieces by a process of natural selection as long as you abide by the rules. My offcuts are managed in this way at the moment. I have been using an old plastic swing bin without the lid. The trouble with this is that all the shorter bits get lost in the bottom of the bin, but what it has done is keep the salvage down to a minimum.

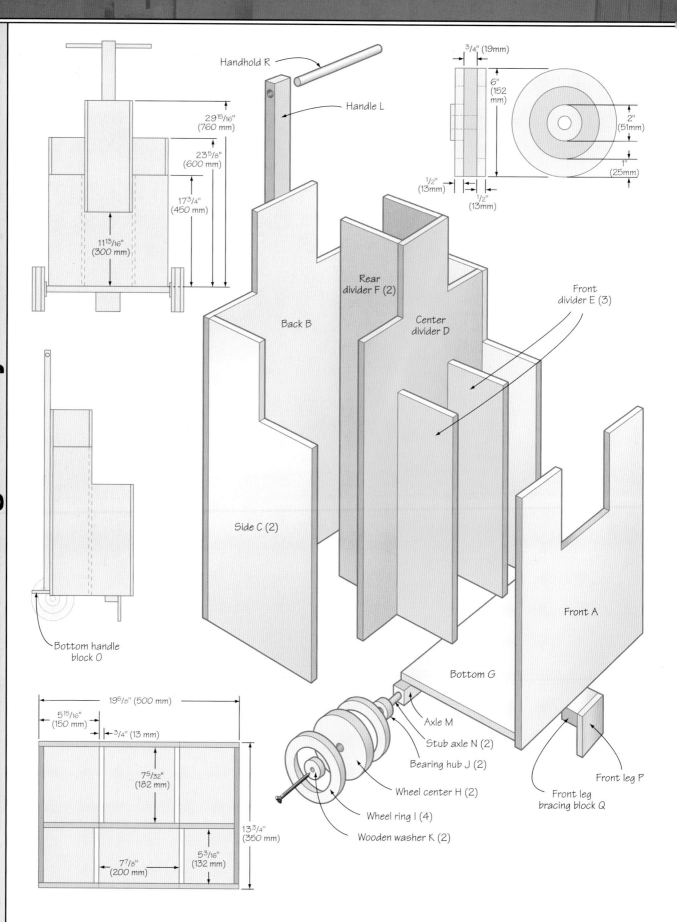

Handhold R

Handle L

29¹⁵/₁₆"
(760 mm)

23⁵/₈"
(600 mm)

17³/₄"
(450 mm)

11¹³/₁₆"
(300 mm)

³/₄" (19mm)

6"
(152
mm)

2"
(51mm)

1"
(25mm)

¹/₂"
(13mm)

¹/₂"
(13mm)

Rear
divider F (2)

Back B

Center
divider D

Front
divider E (3)

Side C (2)

Front A

Bottom handle
block O

Bottom G

Axle M

Stub axle N (2)

Bearing hub J (2)

Wheel center H (2)

Wheel ring I (4)

Wooden washer K (2)

Front leg P

Front leg
bracing block Q

19⁵/₈" (500 mm)

5¹⁵/₁₆"
(150 mm)

³/₄" (13 mm)

7⁵/₃₂"
(182 mm)

7⁷/₈"
(200 mm)

5³/₁₆"
(132 mm)

13³/₄"
(350 mm)

small offcuts storage trolley · inches (millimeters)

REFERENCE	QUANTITY	PART	STOCK	THICKNESS		WIDTH		LENGTH		COMMENTS
A	1	front	MDF	1/2	(12)	19¹¹/₁₆	(500)	17³/₄	(451)	
B	1	back	MDF	1/2	(12)	19¹¹/₁₆	(500)	29¹/₂	(749)	
C	2	sides	MDF	1/2	(12)	12³/₄	(324)	23⁵/₈	(600)	
D	1	center divider	MDF	1/2	(12)	18¹¹/₁₆	(475)	29¹/₂	(749)	
E	2	front dividers	MDF	1/2	(12)	5³/₁₆	(132)	17³/₄	(451)	
F	2	rear dividers	MDF	1/2	(12)	7	(178)	29¹/₂	(749)	
G	1	bottom	MDF	1/2	(12)	13³/₄	(349)	19¹¹/₁₆	(500)	
H	2	wheel centers	MDF	3/4	(18)	6 d	(152)			
I	1	wheel rings	MDF	1/2	(12)	6 d	(152)			
J	2	bearing hubs	hardwood	1	(25)	2 d	(51)			
K	2	wooden washers	hardwood	1	(25)	2 d	(51)			
L	1	handle	2x3 pine	1¹/₂	(38)	2¹/₂	(64)	39³/₈	(1000)	
M	1	axle	2x3 pine	1¹/₂	(38)	1¹/₂	(38)	20³/₄	(527)	
N	2	stub axles	hardwood	3/4 d	(19)			5¹/₂	(140)	
O	1	bottom handle block	MDF	1/2	(12)	2¹/₂	(64)	4¹/₂	(114)	
P	1	front leg	MDF	1/2	(12)	2¹/₂	(64)	3³/₄	(95)	
Q	1	front leg bracing block	2x3 pine	1¹/₂	(38)	2¹/₂	(64)	3	(76)	
R	1	handhold	hardwood	3/4 d	(19)			12	(305)	

hardware & supplies

75 No. 8 × 2" (50mm)
carcass screws

1 Existing storage is a long way from being described as user friendly.

2 Cut the center divider and back to shape using a template and a router setup with a straight-cutting bit and a guide bearing.

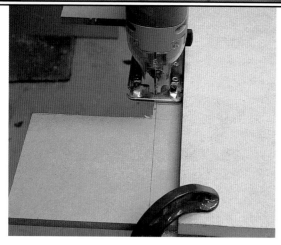

3 Cut the sides and front panel to shape using a jig-saw. Use a straightedge to help guide the jigsaw.

4 Using carcass screws, attach the sides and rear dividers to the back.

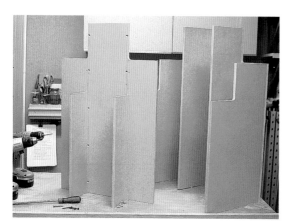

5 Attach the front dividers to the center partition.

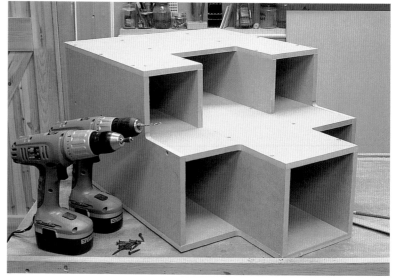

6 Lay the unit on its back and attach the sides. Then attach the front.

7 Attach the bottom.

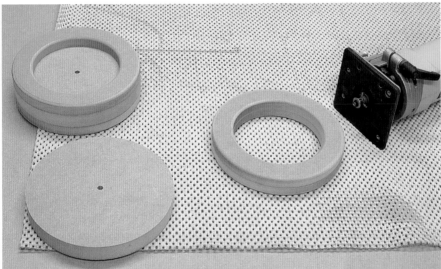

8 Set the drill press to its slowest speed. Secure the adjustable hole cutter in the drill press chuck and adjust it so that it will cut a disc 6" (152mm) in diameter. Cut two discs from $\frac{3}{4}$"-thick (18mm) and four discs from $\frac{1}{2}$"-thick (12mm) MDF. This will make two wheels. Reset the hole cutter to a 4" (102mm) diameter and cut the center out of the $\frac{1}{2}$"-thick (12mm) discs to form rings.

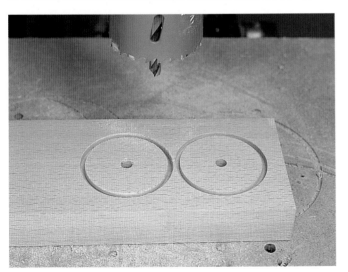

9 With the drill press still set at its slowest speed use a sawtooth cutter to core out two bearing hubs of hardwood.

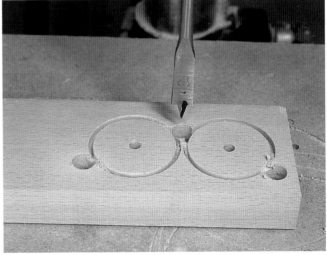

10 One trick you might want to try is drilling waste clearance holes. This will keep the cutting waste wood from clogging up and burning. Before you get all the way through, flip the block over and finish the cut from the other side.

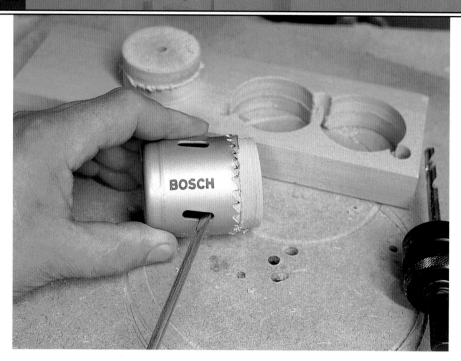

11 Remove the core from the hole saw by prying it out using a screwdriver. Fit the cores onto a long bolt and secure them with a washer and nut. Then chuck the assembly in the drill press and sand it.

12 Assemble two wheels by gluing rings to one disc, one on each side, and the bearing hub to the center on one side only—this will be the inside of the wheel. If you want to paint the "tires" to look like the real thing, feel free. Mine are staying natural with just a coat of sanding sealer.

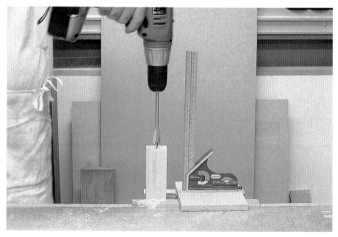

13 The wheels run on stub axles fitted into the ends of a length of timber screwed to the rear bottom of the box. Mortise the dowel stub axles into the ends of the length of timber. This is the trickiest bit of the whole operation. The holes need to be made perfectly parallel to the timber, otherwise the wheels will not be true and will look wonky. Use a combination square as a guide to square the timber in a vise and to line up the drill.

14 Glue the stub axles into place and lubricate them with candle wax.

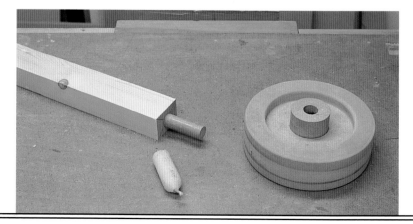

15 Cut 2 wooden discs to use as washers. Use a disc and a screw to hold each wheel onto the stub axle.

16 Using screws, attach the front leg and blocking and the wheel assembly to the bottom of the trolley.

18 Add some measuring marks to the back of the handle, starting at the bottom. Use the bottom handle block as a stop to measure the rough length of your offcuts.

17 Drill a hole in the top of the handle and glue the handhold in place. Using glue and screws, attach the handle assembly to the rear of the storage box. Attach the bottom handle block to the handle assembly.

wall-hung cabinet

Let's face it,

we all love new tools—even if they are just old ones we have newly acquired. The trouble is they all need somewhere to live. In my shed, the planes have spent the past couple of years at the back of the bench under the window. This is far from ideal; they are usually in the way and must be moved from place to place.

The toolbox is good for storing larger tools, but the marking tools and planes need to be close at hand as they are in constant use. A cabinet for the planes and marking tools is a good idea, but finding somewhere to keep the

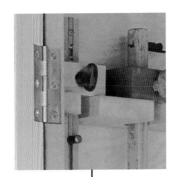

cabinet can be a challenge. After a bit of solo debating—the best kind because I always win—it was unanimously decided to sacrifice some wall space that I had been using to post my schedules, drawings and notes.

To say that space is a bit tight in my shed is an understatement. A conventional door on a cabinet this size would just get in the way. By splitting the door down the middle, the problem is quite literally halved. The doors' frame and panel construction keeps their weight down, which puts less strain on the wall fixings when the doors are open.

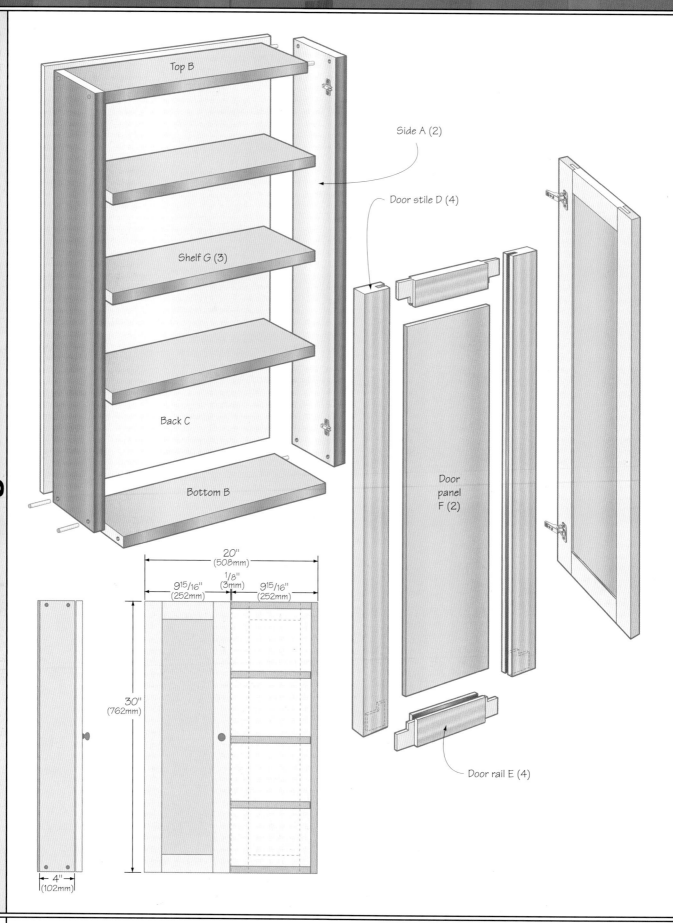

Top B

Side A (2)

Shelf G (3)

Door stile D (4)

Back C

Door panel F (2)

Bottom B

Door rail E (4)

20"
(508mm)

9 15/16"
(252mm)

1/8"
(3mm)

9 15/16"
(252mm)

30"
(762mm)

4"
(102mm)

wall-hung cabinet inches (millimeters)

REFERENCE	QUANTITY	PART	STOCK	THICKNESS		WIDTH		LENGTH		COMMENTS
A	2	sides	MDF	3/4	(18)	2 1/2	(64)	30	(762)	
B	2	top and bottom	MDF	3/4	(18)	2 1/2	(64)	18 1/2	(470)	
C	1	back	plywood	3/8	(9)	20	(508)	30	(762)	
D	4	door stiles	hardwood	3/4	(18)	2	(51)	30	(762)	
E	4	door rails	plywood	3/4	(18)	2	(51)	7 1/2	(191)	
F	2	door panels	plywood	1/4	(6)	6 1/2	(165)	26 1/2	(673)	
G	3	shelves	MDF	3/4	(18)	2	(51)	18 7/16	(468)	

hardware & supplies

4 2¼" (57mm) hinges

8 Miller® dowels

2 1" (25mm) wooden knobs

1 Cut the cabinet parts to size. Then drill holes into the end of the cabinet for the dowels. You may need to use clamps to hold the parts in place during this assembly.

2 Apply a little glue to each dowel and push it as far as it will go using hand pressure. Tap it home using a hammer.

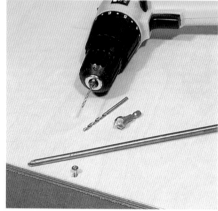

3 When the glue has dried, cut the dowel off just above the surface. Then plane the excess down until it is flush.

4 The back is cut to be just oversized. Then it's screwed to the cabinet along one of the long edges.

5 Turn the cabinet over and check for square. When it's square, clamp it in position, turn over the assembly, and install the screws. After the screws have been inserted, remove the clamps and plane the back or trim it flush with the outside of the cabinet.

6 Make the doors using frame-and-panel construction. After you cut the frame parts to size, cut a groove down the center of each part.

7 Cut the grooves in both the stiles and the rails.

8 Cut the mortises in the stiles.

9 On the ends of the rails, cut and fit the tenons to the mortises. Cut a haunch in the tenons so you can have a longer tenon and still keep the groove for the panel at a smaller depth.

10 Have your clamps ready, then apply glue to the tenons and assemble the doors.

11 Once the doors are glued and clamped, check them for square, set them on a level surface, and let the glue cure.

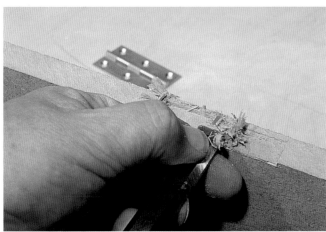

12 Chiseling the mortises in the edge of the cabinet is unconventional because it means cutting them into the end grain of the MDF. The best way I have found to do this is to score around the hinge with a knife to the depth of the mortise and then gauge a line to the depth required. Chip down into the cut, opening the cut line out to a V that extends into the waste. Then carefully pare down the rest of the waste to the gauge line. Use a very sharp chisel for this, and try not to break out the back of the mortise.

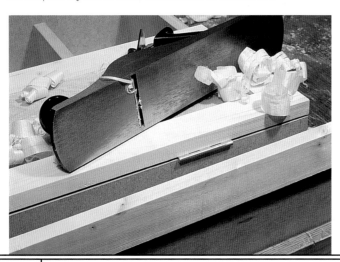

13 Attach the hinges to the cabinet.

14 Rest the doors on the face of the cabinet and trim them to fit. A bit of time spent here carefully planing the doors to fit is a good investment. Use the cabinet as a gauge to fit the doors. When you are satisfied that the doors fit correctly with a nice even gap between them, you can hang them.

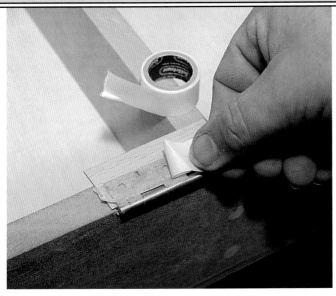

15 Support the hinge with a thin piece of cardboard or a piece of veneer to stop it from closing completely. Then apply a strip of double-stick tape to each hinge.

16 Place the doors back on top and arrange them in their final position. Press down at the hinge positions to stick the hinges to the doors. Open each door in turn and scribe the hinge positions with a knife.

17 Separate the hinge from the door and chop the mortise's waste.

18 Cut the mortises on the door in the conventional way and hang the doors. They will fit perfectly!

19 Fit a couple of wooden knobs on the doors and hang the cabinet on the wall similar to the router cutters cabinet. See page 35, "Hanging the cabinet". Fill it with planes, marking tools or other tools of your choice.

downdraft table

What is the worst job

in the workshop? For me it is cleaning up all the dust produced by sawing, routing and sanding. A good power tool extractor can help, but it will collect only the dust right from the power tool and allow some dust to get blasted into the environment. Given time, air cleaners will remove dust from the air; keeping the dust out of the air in the first place is even better.

To prevent dust from being blown all over the workshop, we need to create an airflow that will guide the dust where we want it to go. To create a downdraft all we need to do is to create lower pressure below the bench than above it. The theory may be simple, but putting it in practice requires some thought.

The downdraft table is basically an empty box with lots of holes in the top and an extractor plugged into the bottom. The idea is to work on top of the table and let the airflow draw any extraneous dust down into the void below, through the hose and into the collection bin or bag of the extractor.

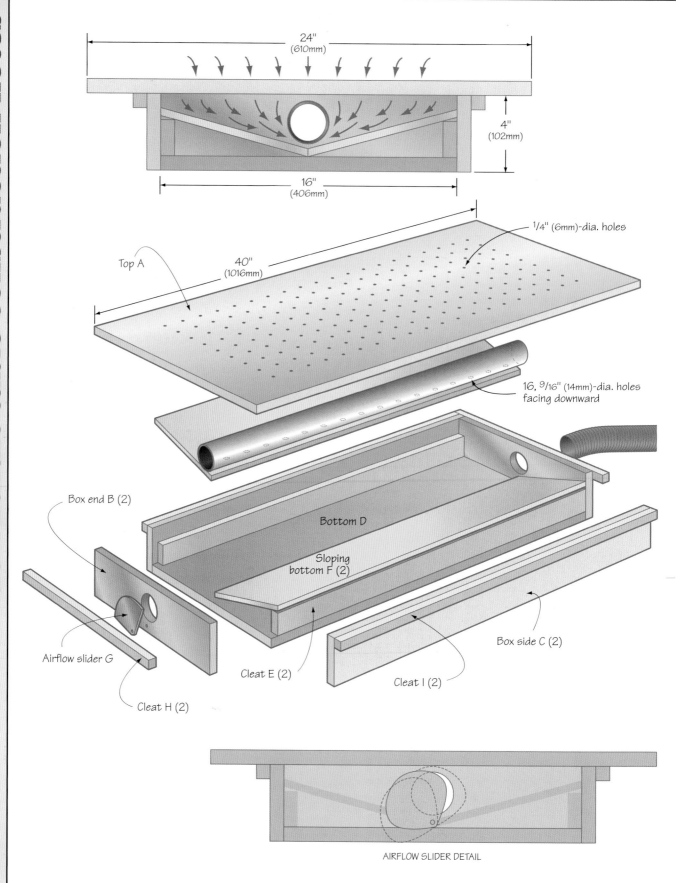

24"
(610mm)

4"
(102mm)

16"
(406mm)

1/4" (6mm)-dia. holes

Top A

40"
(1016mm)

16, 9/16" (14mm)-dia. holes
facing downward

Box end B (2)

Bottom D

Sloping
bottom F (2)

Box side C (2)

Airflow slider G

Cleat E (2)

Cleat I (2)

Cleat H (2)

AIRFLOW SLIDER DETAIL

downdraft table inches (millimeters)

REFERENCE	QUANTITY	PART	STOCK	THICKNESS		WIDTH		LENGTH		COMMENTS
A	1	top	MDF	3/4	(18)	23¹/2	(597)	47¹/2	(1207)	
B	2	box ends	MDF	3/4	(18)	4	(102)	14¹/2	(368)	
C	2	box sides	MDF	3/4	(18)	4	(102)	40	(1016)	
D	1	bottom	MDF	3/4	(18)	14¹/2	(368)	38¹/2	(978)	
E	2	cleats	MDF	3/4	(18)	2¹/2	(64)	38¹/2	(978)	
F	2	sloping bottoms	MDF	3/8	(9)	7¹/8	(181)	38¹/2	(978)	
G	1	airflow slider	MDF	1/4	(6)	3	(76)	3	(76)	
H	2	cleats	hardwood	1/4	(6)	3/4	(19)	17¹/2	(445)	
I	2	cleats	hardwood	1/4	(6)	3/4	(19)	40	(1016)	

hardware & supplies

1/4" (6mm) x 3/4"
(18mm) x 13' (4m)
hardwood edging for top

109" (277cm) strip insulation

2¹/4" (57mm)-diameter x
40" (1016mm) plastic pipe

1 1¹/4" (32mm)-20 x 1¹/4"
(32mm) bolt

1 1¹/4" (32mm)-20 wingnut

24" (610mm) x 48" (1219mm)
high-pressure laminate

1 Edge the MDF with a hardwood edging to help keep the table in good condition. This downdraft table is going to be a benchtop item. The size of the table will vary depending on your expected use. If you are only making small boxes, for example, then a small, compact version will do the trick. As most of my building is furniture of one kind or another I have decided to build this one with a table size of 48" × 24" (1219mm × 610mm). This is large enough to accommodate most parts that will need sanding or routing.

2 Apply contact cement to both the tabletop and bottom of the laminate.

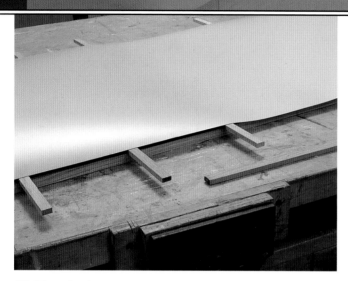

3 When the glue is dry to the touch, lay sticks to aid positioning. Remove the center stick first and work your way out to the ends. This prevents air from being trapped under the laminate.

4 Use a J-roller to apply even pressure on the laminate.

5 Using a trim router with a bevel cutter and a guide bearing, trim the laminate flush with the edges of the tabletop.

6 Using a straight-edge and a soft pencil, draw a grid on the tabletop. This will help you see where to drill the draft holes.

7 You can drill the holes freehand, but this hardwood drilling guide will keep the holes lined up straight. Drill a hole in the block that lines up with the intersection of the grid lines when a straightedge is set on a grid line. Rest the tabletop on a piece of scrap sheet material and bore the holes through the tabletop and into the scrap. This will reduce the tear-out on the underside of the tabletop.

8 Cut the parts for the box, then glue and screw them together.

back to school

Because we are dealing with fine, fast-moving dust in relatively small quantities we need to keep the air velocity high to be effective. My dust extractor (vacuum) has a specified air-flow of 116.53 CF/Minute (3300 L/Minute). Fitted with a 2¼"-diameter (57mm) hose, the air speed is quite acceptable. In order to maintain that speed the total area of the holes open to the atmosphere must equal the area of the hose opening.

Here's the math bit—now don't rush off; it's not that bad. It is worked here in metric. The area of a circle is πr^2, where $\pi = 3.142$ and $r^2 =$ radius × radius. The sectional area of the hose is calculated as follows:

$$3.142 \times (57mm \div 2)^2$$
$$= \quad 3.142 \times 812.25$$
$$= \quad 2552 \text{ sq. mm}$$

By the same formula, the area of a 5mm-diameter hole is 19.6375 sq. mm. Divide the sectional area of the hose by the area of one hole to get the optimum number of holes, which is 130 holes (2552 ÷ 19.6375).

For those of you that work in inches and feet, the equivalent calculations follow:

$$3.142 \times (2.25" \div 2)^2$$
$$= \quad 3.142 \times 1.2656$$
$$= \quad 3.9765 \text{ sq. in. (rounded to 4 sq. in.)}$$

The area of a .25"-diameter hole is .049 sq. in.

The number of ¼"-diameter holes needed is 82 (4 ÷ .049). A ¼"-diameter hole is 1.6 times larger in area than a 5mm hole, therefore, less holes are needed.

My table has 189, 5mm holes. Assuming that some of the holes are covered by the workpiece, this will work efficiently.

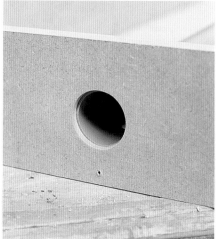

9 Glue the cleats and the sloping sections in place to create an airtight seal.

10 See the illustration for locating the holes for the plastic pipe. Cut the holes for the pipe using a hole saw of the appropriate size.

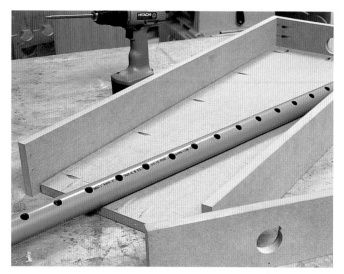

11 Bore 16 holes, each with a $9/16"$ (14mm) diameter, down the pipe's length. This is about the same area as the extractor's hose and will ensure an even draft throughout the box. Fit the pipe with the holes on the underside into the holes at each end of the box. Trim the ends of the pipe flush with the box.

12 The airflow slider consists of a quadrant of thin MDF which pivots on a bolt and is secured in position by a wing nut. Position the airflow slider at one end. Plug the extractor hose into the opposite end.

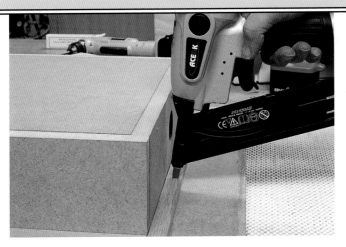

13 Center the tabletop over the box and hold it in place with strips of wood glued and nailed to the underside of the tabletop. Adding strip insulation around the top of the box will help make an airtight seal.

14 To use this downdraft box, secure it to a bench. You can do this in a variety of ways. I stand the unit on a nonslip mat. A batten screwed to the bottom of the unit could be held in a Work-mate® portable bench or your shop bench's vise. Once the unit is secure, place a nonslip mat between the surface and the workpiece. If you are sanding or doing light profiling, the mat will be sufficient.

15 If necessary, use clamps around the overhang to secure the workpiece to the tabletop. If the workpiece is large and covers too many holes, the sound of the extractor will rise in tone and volume, similar to what happens when an obstruction causes a blockage in the hose. To rectify this, open the airflow slider until the tone of the extractor returns to normal.

16 Conversely, if a workpiece is very small, the airflow around it may not be sufficient to clear the waste quickly enough. To rectify this cover a section of the table with a sheet of MDF or something similar to restrict the airflow.

clamp stand

As your collection of

clamps grows, and it will if it hasn't already, storage becomes a more significant issue. The time-honored solution of hanging clamps on the wall is fine if you have the room, but it is not ideal if glue-up will take place in various locations within the work area. An alternative is to build a portable rack to hold the clamps and the glue paraphernalia.

This simple-to-build clamp stand, requiring only basic tools and techniques, is a useful addition to any small workshop. The sizes specified can, of course, be modified to suit individual requirements. If space is at a real premium, you could build two smaller stands to be used and stored individually, without compromising the amount of clamp storage.

clamp stand construction notes

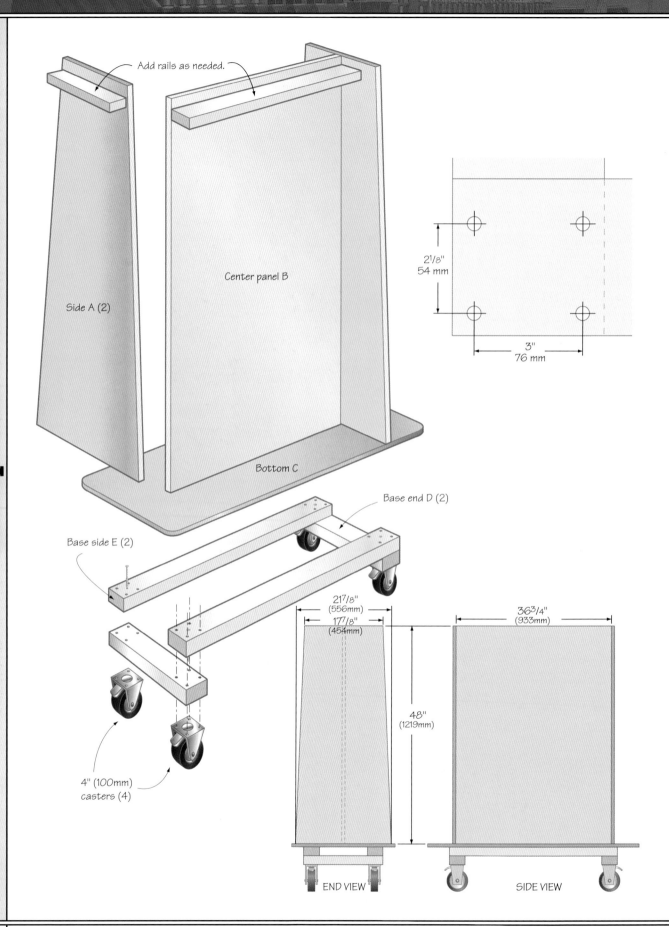

Add rails as needed.

Center panel B

Side A (2)

Bottom C

2¹/8"
54 mm

3"
76 mm

Base end D (2)

Base side E (2)

4" (100mm)
casters (4)

21⁷/8"
(556mm)

17⁷/8"
(454mm)

48"
(1219mm)

36³/4"
(933mm)

END VIEW

SIDE VIEW

clamp stand inches (millimeters)

REFERENCE	QUANTITY	PART	STOCK	THICKNESS		WIDTH		LENGTH		COMMENTS
A	2	sides	MDF	3/4	(18)	21^7/$_8$	(556)	48	(1219)	
B	1	center panel	MDF	3/4	(18)	36^3/$_4$	(933)	48	(1219)	
C	1	bottom	MDF	3/4	(18)	24	(610)	48	(1219)	
D	2	base ends	pine	1^1/$_2$	(38)	3^1/$_2$	(89)	18	(457)	
E	2	base sides	pine	1^1/$_2$	(38)	3^1/$_2$	(89)	38^1/$_4$	(972)	

hardware & supplies

- 4   4"(100mm)-diameter casters
- 16 ^{3}/$_8$"-16 x 3" (M10 x 1.5 x 75mm) carriage bolts
- 16 ^{3}/$_8$" (M10) hex nuts
- 16 ^{3}/$_8$" (M10) flat washers

1 A substantial frame is required to support the weight of many clamps. This will also provide a firm fixing point for the mounting plate of the wheels. On a workshop floor (or the garage or shed floor) any wheels smaller than 4" (100mm) in diameter will get caught on small obstructions.

2 Mark up the ends of the shorter pieces for drilling as shown in the drawing. Vary the dimensions if you are using lumber of a different cross sectional size. Counterbore at the inner marks, using a 1" (25mm) Forstner bit, to a depth of ^{5}/$_8$" (16mm). Continue the holes through, using a ^{3}/$_8$" (10mm) drill bit. Bore the outer holes to ^{3}/$_8$" (10mm).

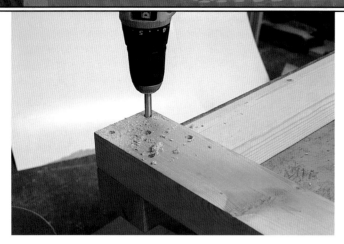

3 Lay the two shorter pieces on the bench and place the longer pieces across them to make a rectangle. Mark the center point of each intersection and bore a countersunk hole for a wood screw. Coat the mating surfaces with glue, and secure the frame at each corner with a 3" (76mm) wood screw. When the glue is dry, extend the outer holes through using a $^3/_8$" (10mm) drill bit and counter-bore to $^5/_8$" (16 mm).

4 Fit each wheel using two 4" (100mm) and two 2" (50mm) coach (carriage) bolts. If you use wider bottom boards, all four holes can be drilled through both base frame pieces. Then you would use four 4" (100mm) carriage bolts to attach each wheel.

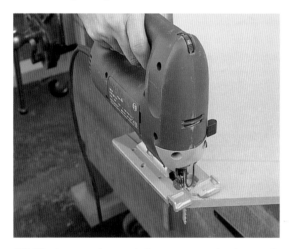

5 The base needs rounded corners to make the stand more user friendly. Make a template from an offcut of sheet material by drawing an arc at one corner and trimming to just outside of the line. Finish down to the line by carefully sanding to the mark.

6 Position the template on the corners of the base and trace the arc. Trim to the outside of the line with a jigsaw. Reposition the template onto the base to ensure that the sides are flush. Using a bearing-guided, flush-trim cutter in a small router or laminate trimmer, machine the corner flush to the template. Repeat for the other three corners.

7 Replace the flush-trim cutter with a roundover cutter and round over the top and bottom surfaces of the base.

8 Cut the parts for the stand and glue and screw them together. Trace the outline of the assembly onto the base and lift the assembly clear. Drill pilot holes through the base. Invert the assembly and position the base, now on top, using the traced alignment marks. Drill through the pilot holes into the assembly and secure with carcass screws. Return the structure to its correct orientation and fasten it to the wheeled frame with screws.

9 Use one side of this stand exclusively for the storage of bar and sash clamps.

10 The other side has a couple of rails added; use these to hang C-clamps and individual clamps. Handscrew clamps and other types of clamps can also be attached to these bars.

mobile table saw stand

Let's assume that you are

a keen woodworker whose work space has to double as something else, such as a garage, a garden shed or an outbuilding. Ideally everything will be portable so that it can be stored in a minimum amount of space and out of the way while not in use.

This is especially challenging with the table saw. A prime consideration is weight—even

with wheels, mobility is an issue—so I have concentrated on contractor's saws.

A contractor's saw is intended for use on a collapsible stand. That method just means the idle saw will take up floor space and the stand will have to be stored too. Besides that, you will have to set up the stand and the saw every time you want to use it. With the mobile table saw stand, you can forget about all that fuss and gain valuable storage space.

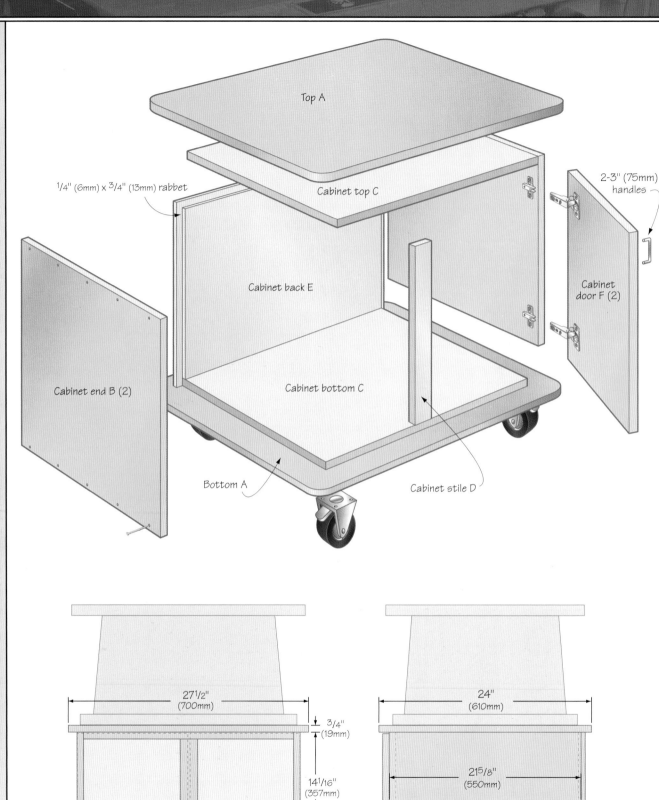

Top A

Cabinet top C

1/4" (6mm) x 3/4" (13mm) rabbet

2-3" (75mm) handles

Cabinet back E

Cabinet door F (2)

Cabinet end B (2)

Cabinet bottom C

Bottom A

Cabinet stile D

27 1/2" (700mm)

3/4" (19mm)

14 1/16" (357mm)

3/4" (19mm)

FRONT VIEW

24" (610mm)

21 5/8" (550mm)

END VIEW

mobile table saw stand inches (millimeters)

REFERENCE	QUANTITY	PART	STOCK	THICKNESS		WIDTH		LENGTH		COMMENTS
A	2	top and bottom	MDF	3/4	(18)	24	(610)	27¹/₂	(700)	
B	2	cabinet ends	MDF	3/4	(18)	14¹/₁₆ h	(357)	21⁵/₈ d	(550)	
C	2	cabinet top and bottom	MDF	3/4	(18)	22	(559)	24	(610)	
D	1	cabinet stile	MDF	3/4	(18)	2	(51)	12¹/₈	(308)	
E	1	cabinet back	MDF	3/4	(18)	13⁵/₈ h	(346)	25¹/₂	(648)	
F	2	doors	MDF	3/4	(18)	12⁵/₈	(321)	13³/₄ h	(349)	

hardware & supplies

4   4"(100mm)-diameter lockable casters

16 3/8"-16 x 1" (M10 x 1.5 x 25mm) carriage bolts

16 3/8" (M10) hex nuts

16 3/8" (M10) flat washers

4   107° European overlay hinges with mounting plates

This is how it used to be. The saw was screwed to a pair of horses through a piece of MDF

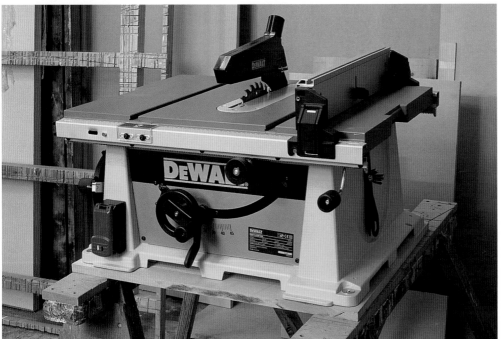

This temporary arrangement is fine for a small amount of cutting. However, it does make it a bit on the high side for every day use and the horses' legs can get in the way when using the saw.

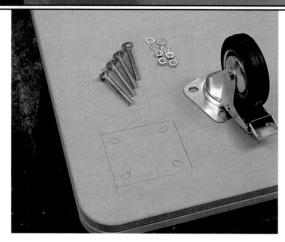

1 Make a rounded-corner template. Mark the corners of the top and bottom pieces using the template as a guide. Remove the bulk of the waste with a jigsaw, and trim to the line using a router fitted with a profiling cutter. Round over the top and bottom edges.

2 Drill holes for mounting the wheels into one of the pieces. I use coach (carriage) bolts to mount the casters. The bolts need to be just long enough to pass through the mounting plate of the wheel plus the base and leave enough thread to secure a nut over a washer.

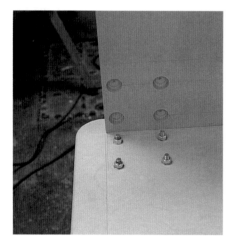

3 Cut out the cabinet parts and bore some clearance holes in the bottom of the cabinet bottom. This will enable you to mount the assembled cabinet flat on the base.

4 Using biscuits, glue and carcass screws, assemble the cabinet sides and top and bottom pieces. Then install the cabinet stile using glue and screws.

5 Cut a ³⁄₄"-wide (18mm) by ¹⁄₄"-deep (6mm) rabbet around the inner face of the back panel to match up with the open carcass.

6 Secure the back with glue and carcass screws. Do not overtighten the screws or the cabinet parts will split.

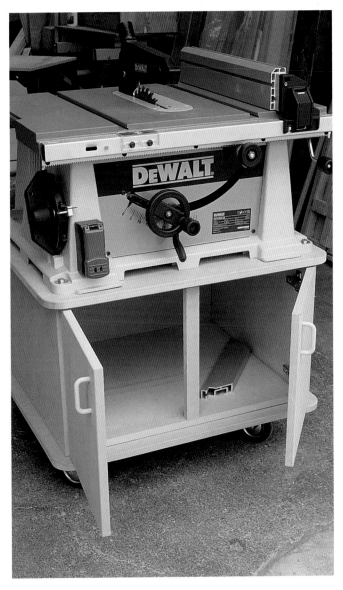

7 The doors are hung on European-style concealed hinges. Drill the cup holes in the doors for the hinges using a drill press. Fix the hinge mounting plates to the inside of the carcass and hang the doors. Fit on the doors a pair of handles, rather than knobs that may catch on something.

8 Turn the assembled cabinet upside down. Attach the bottom by locating the wheel-securing nuts in the previously drilled clearance holes and secure the wheeled base to the cabinet with screws. Turn the unit back up the correct way and lock the wheels.

Mark the position of the saw on the top and, using a 1" (25mm) Forstner bit, bore a ¹⁄₈"-deep (3mm) recess at each of the hole positions. Follow through with a ⁷⁄₁₆" (11mm) hole. Set a T-nut into each recess from inside the cabinet. Do not hammer these in; it is far better to pull these home using a wrench and a couple of washers to spread the load.

Put the saw on top of the cabinet (you will most likely need an assistant to do this!), aligning the bolts through the mounting holes in the saw's base. Install washers and nuts on the bolts and tighten them to hold the saw securely in place.

If the table saw you are using does not have a place to store the cable, make simple wind-around storage hooks and affix them to the back of the cabinet.

outfeed table

No matter how large a

workshop is you can never have enough space. Floor space is always at a premium in an environment that is constantly changing: Lumber stocks vary, the waste (those might-come-in-handy-one-day offcuts) starts occupying more space than the stock lumber, projects under construction need somewhere to sit and the occasional new piece of equipment has to be squeezed in!

One casualty of my space problem has been the router table. A permanent router cabinet, one that supports a custom-made router table and a fence and has the storage space of an aircraft hanger, had been in my "planning department" for more years than I care to remember. Its development was thwarted by the advantages of using a router tabletop mounted

on a pair of collapsible workbenches—even though that approach cost each project a lot of setup time.

My space problem also led to unsatisfactory working practice at the cabinet saw. Every time I wanted to rip something down I had to figure out how to support the work at the outfeed. I have used something that is collapsible, which has meant more setup time.

My solution to these problems was inspirated by the combination woodworking machine—one space, multiple uses.

An outfeed table with lockable casters can be used for other purposes—an assembly table or just a flat surface on which to lay out the components of a job. Cut a recess in one end for a router mounting plate, and two of the workshop's logistical problems have been solved in one go.

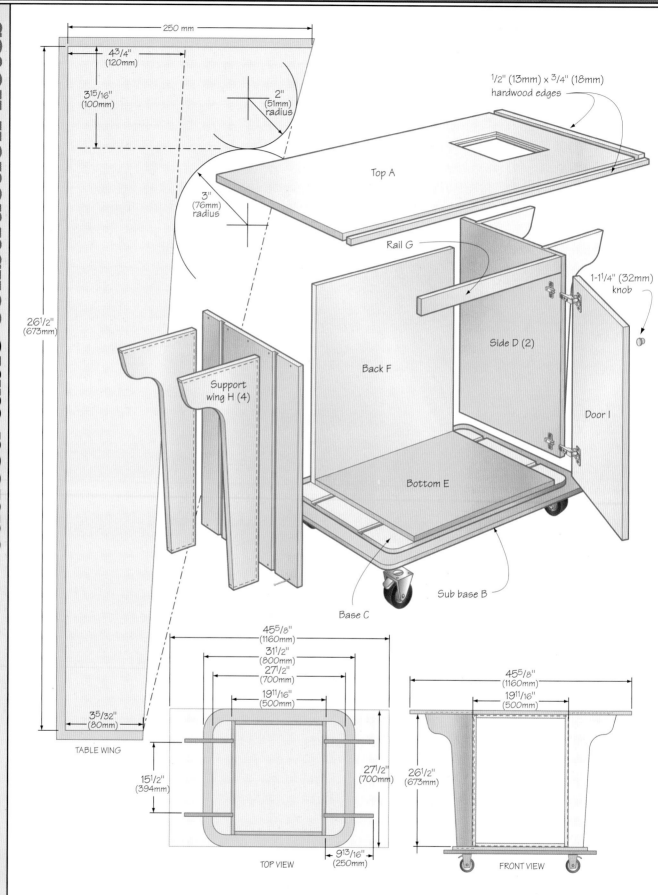

250 mm

4³/4"
(120mm)

3¹⁵/16"
(100mm)

2"
(51mm)
radius

3"
(76mm)
radius

¹/2" (13mm) x ³/4" (18mm)
hardwood edges

Top A

Rail G

Side D (2)

1-1¹/4" (32mm)
knob

Back F

26¹/2"
(673mm)

Support
wing H (4)

Door I

Bottom E

Base C

Sub base B

3⁵/32"
(80mm)

TABLE WING

45⁵/8"
(1160mm)

31¹/2"
(800mm)

27¹/2"
(700mm)

19¹¹/16"
(500mm)

15¹/2"
(394mm)

27¹/2"
(700mm)

9¹³/16"
(250mm)

TOP VIEW

45⁵/8"
(1160mm)

19¹¹/16"
(500mm)

26¹/2"
(673mm)

FRONT VIEW

outfeed table inches (millimeters)

REFERENCE	QUANTITY	PART	STOCK	THICKNESS		WIDTH		LENGTH		COMMENTS
A	1	top	MDF	$3/4$	(18)	$27^1/2$	(700)	$45^5/8$	(1160)	
B	1	sub base	MDF	$3/4$	(18)	$27^1/2$	(700)	$31^1/2$	(800)	
C	1	base	MDF	$3/4$	(18)	$23^5/8$	(600)	$27^1/2$	(700)	
D	2	sides	MDF	$3/4$	(18)	$23^3/4$	(603)	$26^1/2$	(673)	
E	1	bottom	MDF	$3/4$	(18)	$18^1/8$	(460)	$22^{13}/16$	(580)	
F	1	back	MDF	$3/4$	(18)	$19^{11}/16$	(500)	$26^1/2$	(673)	
G	1	rail	MDF	$3/4$	(18)	4	(102)	$18^1/8$	(460)	
H	4	support wings	MDF	$3/4$	(18)	$9^{13}/16$	(250)	$26^1/2$	(673)	
I	1	door	MDF	$3/4$	(18)	$19^{11}/16$	(500)	26	(660)	

hardware & supplies

- 4 4"(100mm)-diameter castors
- 16 $3/8$"-16 x 1"(M10 x 1.5 x 25mm) carriage bolts
- 16 $3/8$" (M10) hex nuts
- 16 $3/8$"(M10) flat washers
  29"(740mm) x 47"(1200mm) high-pressure laminate
- 4 170° European hinges with mounting plates

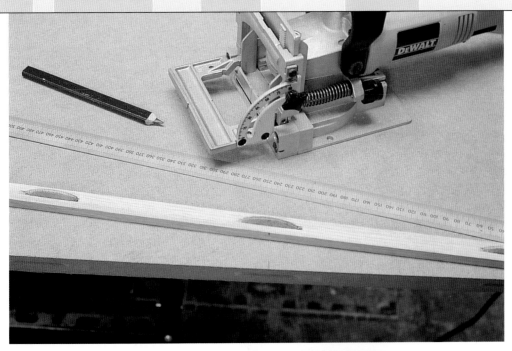

1 Cut the top to size according to the cutting list and edge it with strips of hardwood using No. 0 biscuits and glue to secure the hardwood trim on the edges of the top.

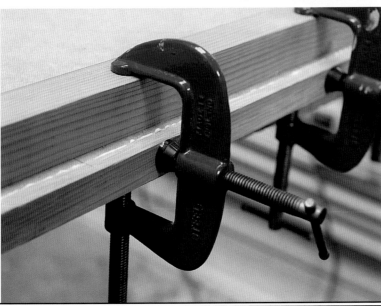

2 Edging cramps (clamps) are used to secure the hardwood trim. When the glue has cured, laminate the top surface, including the hardwood edges.

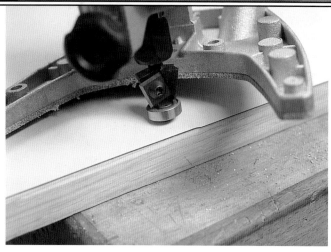

3 Trim the edges with a flush-trim cutter or, as shown here, with a bearing-guided chamfer cutter. The chamfer will prevent the top from being damaged by something catching the edge of the laminate.

4 Lay out the shape of the wings and make a template.

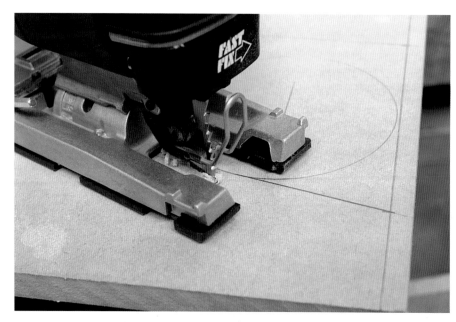

5 Cut out the template and sand the curves smooth. Use this template to rout four wings. Then round over the curved, outside edges of the wings using a router and a roundover cutter.

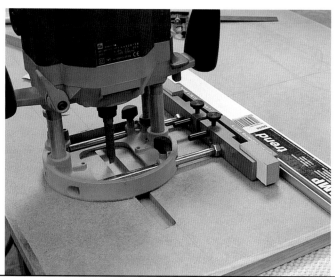

6 Cut the dadoes in the underside of the top. Make these just a little wider than the thickness of the wings and sides. This will help with the assembly process. Use this same process to cut the dadoes in the sides.

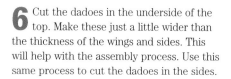

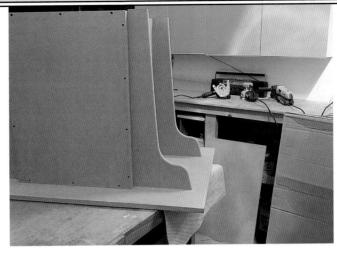

7 Assemble the cabinet and round over its outside edges. Mark the position of the grooves to be cut in the cabinet by setting it on the overturned top. Then cut the grooves in the cabinet sides.

8 Using glue and screws, attach the cabinet to its top, taking care to align the grooves. Apply glue in the grooves, set the wings into them and toenail them to the cabinet.

10 Drill the cup holes for the European hinges, hang the door and install a knob. If you want to use this as a router table, make in one end of the top the recessed cut for the router mounting plate.

9 Cut out the larger bottom, and round the corners using a template and a router. Locate the casters on the bottom; trace and drill the mounting holes for the casters. Cut out the smaller base, center it on the larger base plate, and clamp it in place. Using the larger base as a template, mark the location of the mounting holes on the smaller base.

Use a 1"-diameter (25mm) Forstner bit to bore 1/2"-deep (13mm) blind holes into the smaller piece where you marked the mounting hole location. These will give enough clearance for the protruding fixings or bolts. Do not assemble the two pieces yet.

Lay the smaller piece, blind holes down, on a flat surface and place the cabinet carcass on it in its correct orientation. Mark the position of the dadoes for the side supports and wings. Cut the dadoes using the router setup as you did in step 6.

Attach the small bottom to the cabinet using glue and screws. Attach the casters to the larger base, then attach that to the smaller base using glue and screws.

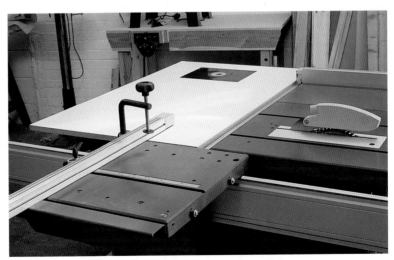

11 The MDF will absorb moisture and all sorts of stains if it is not sealed. Do this by painting or, as I have done; applying a couple of coats of sanding sealer. Finish the plastic laminate top with furniture polish. This will help the project materials slide over the surface with minimum resistance.

freestanding cabinet

Storage in the workshop

needs to be practical and flexible. To this end, a lot of the principles used in kitchen cabinets can be employed. Good-quality secondhand kitchen units are useful if they are in tip-top condition. Skip the ill-fitting shabby cabinets—a workshop that has interior design concepts inspired by the local dump will just feel cluttered. I have a few secondhand kitchen cabinets that I have had for over 25 years, but I don't have enough of them to accommodate all the things that need storing.

Rather than trying to imitate high-quality mass-produced cabinets, I have embarked on building a cabinet system that looks totally different from the commercial offerings. I have also taken a modular approach so the units can be moved around somewhat easily.

Using the European system as a basis, the entire cabinet system is based on modules that are $19^5/8"$ (500mm) wide. The cabinet in this project is a double-base unit that is $39^1/4"$ (1000mm) wide. All the base units will be $18^3/16"$ (460mm) deep and $33^7/8"$ (860mm) high. The units stand on a 4"-high (100mm) plinth and have false backs that are set in grooves 2" (50mm) from the rear of the sides.

The space at the back of the cabinet will allow the cabinet to be scribed and cut to fit against an uneven wall. Cords or other services can be run behind the cabinets or through the plinth.

The front of the carcass has a face frame planted onto it. The raised-panel doors are hung within the face frame using butt hinges, and the drawers are beaded top and bottom and sit flush within the face frame.

freestanding cabinet construction notes

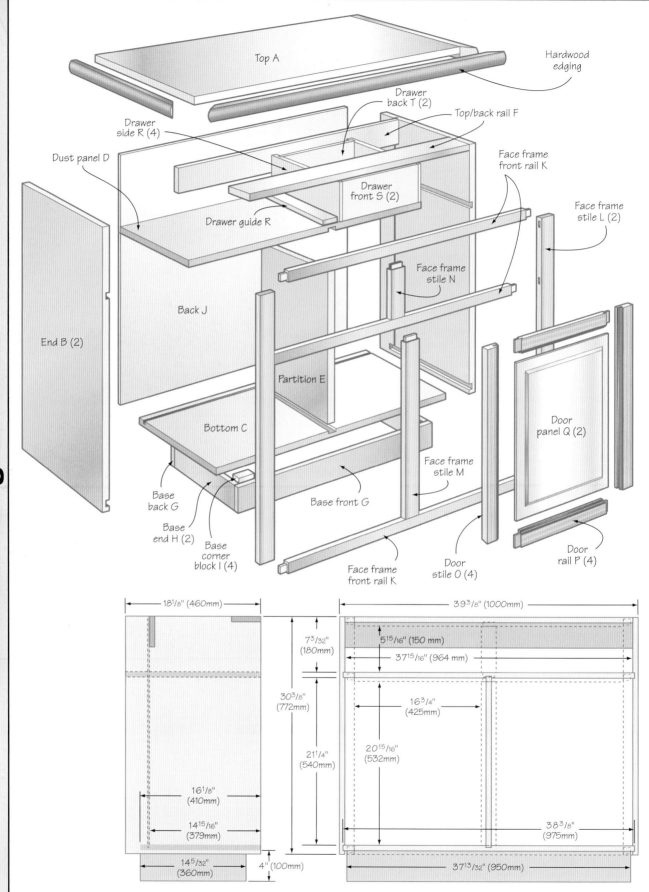

Top A

Hardwood edging

Drawer back T (2)

Top/back rail F

Drawer side R (4)

Dust panel D

Face frame front rail K

Face frame stile L (2)

Drawer front S (2)

Drawer guide R

Face frame stile N

Back J

End B (2)

Partition E

Door panel Q (2)

Bottom C

Base back G

Face frame stile M

Base end H (2)

Base front G

Base corner block I (4)

Door stile O (4)

Door rail P (4)

Face frame front rail K

18¹/₈" (460mm)

39³/₈" (1000mm)

7³/₃₂" (180mm)

5¹⁵/₁₆" (150 mm)

37¹⁵/₁₆" (964 mm)

30³/₈" (772mm)

16³/₄" (425mm)

20¹⁵/₁₆" (532mm)

21¹/₄" (540mm)

16¹/₈" (410mm)

14¹⁵/₁₆" (379mm)

38³/₈" (975mm)

14⁵/₃₂" (360mm)

4" (100mm)

37¹³/₃₂" (950mm)

freestanding cabinet inches (millimeters)

REFERENCE	QUANTITY	PART	STOCK	THICKNESS		WIDTH		LENGTH		COMMENTS
A	1	top	pine	$1^1/_2$	(38)	$19^{11}/_{16}$	(500)	$41^3/_8$	(1051)	
B	2	ends	MDF	$3/_4$	(18)	$18^3/_{32}$	(460)	$30^3/_8$	(772)	
C	1	bottom	MDF	$3/_4$	(18)	$18^3/_{32}$	(460)	$38^{13}/_{32}$	(976)	
D	1	dust panel	MDF	$3/_4$	(18)	$16^1/_8$	(410)	$38^{13}/_{32}$	(976)	
E	1	partition	MDF	$3/_4$	(18)	$16^1/_8$	(410)	$21^7/_8$	(556)	
F	2	top and back rails	MDF	$3/_4$	(18)	4	(100)	$37^{15}/_{16}$	(964)	
G	2	base front and back	MDF	$3/_4$	(18)	4	(100)	$37^{13}/_{32}$	(950)	
H	2	base ends	MDF	$3/_4$	(18)	4	(100)	$12^3/_4$	(324)	
I	4	base corner blocks	MDF	$3/_4$	(18)	4	(100)	4	(100)	
J	1	back	MDF	$1/_4$	(6)	$29^{15}/_{32}$	(748)	$38^{13}/_{32}$	(976)	
K	3	face frame rails	pine	$3/_4$	(19)	$1^3/_{16}$	(30)	$37^{13}/_{32}$	(950)	tenons on both ends
L	2	face frame stiles	pine	$3/_4$	(19)	2	(50)	$30^3/_8$	(772)	
M	1	face frame stile	pine	$3/_4$	(19)	2	(50)	$21^7/_8$	(556)	tenons on both ends
N	1	face frame stile	pine	$3/_4$	(19)	2	(50)	$6^{13}/_{16}$	(174)	tenons on both ends
O	4	door stiles	pine	$3/_4$	(19)	$2^{11}/_{32}$	(60)	$21^9/_{32}$	(540)	
P	4	door rails	pine	$3/_4$	(19)	$2^{11}/_{32}$	(60)	$13^{11}/_{32}$	(339)	
Q	2	door panels	pine	$9/_{16}$	(14)	$13^3/_{32}$	(333)	$17^5/_8$	(448)	
R	4	drawer sides	pine	$1/_2$	(13)	$5^{13}/_{16}$	(148)	$16^9/_{16}$	(421)	
S	2	drawer fronts	pine	$1/_2$	(13)	$5^{13}/_{16}$	(148)	$16^{23}/_{32}$	(425)	
T	2	drawer backs	pine	$1/_2$	(13)	$5^5/_{16}$	(135)	$16^7/_{32}$	(412)	
U	2	drawer bottoms	plywood	$1/_4$	(6)	$16^7/_{32}$	(412)	$15^{23}/_{32}$	(399)	
V	4	drawer slips	pine	$1/_2$	(13)	$3/_4$	(19)	$15^3/_8$	(391)	

hardware & supplies

4 $1^1/_4$" (32mm) wooden knobs

4 $2^1/_2$" (64mm) butt hinges

1 Nominal 1" × 6" (25mm × 150mm) boards are ready for rough cutting to length after spending a week in the workshop acclimating. A hand saw is the quickest way to cut long boards in a short workshop!

2 Rip the boards to width using a table saw.

3 Large sheets can be easily cut into manageable pieces using a circular saw and a straightedge clamped in place.

4 After cutting all parts to size as shown in the cutting list, mark the locations of the dadoes in the cabinet sides, drawer sides, etc., and rout them. You may need to adjust the width of the grooves slighty to accept the panels that fit into them. It's almost impossible to find a router bit that is just the right size.

5 Assemble the cabinet using glue and screws. Be sure the screw hole is big enough or you could split the MDF. Or, if the hole is too big your screw might not hold properly.

6 Using glue and screws, assemble the plinth (base).

7 Cut the face frame components to length. Then cut the mortises, and cut and fit the tenons.

8 Glue and clamp the frame together, ensuring that it is square and not twisted. Let the glue dry.

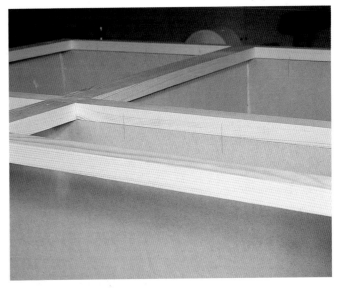

9 Attach the face frame to the face of the carcass using No. 20 biscuits. Temporarily clamp the frame to the carcass and mark the position of the biscuit slots. Remove the frame and cut the slots in the carcass. To make cutting the slots in the frame much easier, flip the frame and clamp it back onto the carcass. Cut the biscuit slots, ensuring that the carcass is not proud of the frame where the slot is being cut, as this will affect the alignment. Paint a coat of polyvinyl acetate glue (PVA) onto the front edge of the carcass and let it dry for about 15 minutes. Glue up the face frame and paint all the biscuits with glue before inserting them in the slots. The MDF on the carcass will have soaked up the first coat of glue, so apply a second coat and fit the face frame to the carcass. Use plenty of clamps to hold it in place.

10 The face frame is attached to the carcass so that the top of the rails align with the dust panel and the bottom.

11 Cut the profile on one edge of all the door parts.

12 Use a profiled push block as a backer to prevent breakout while cutting the scribe on the ends of the stiles.

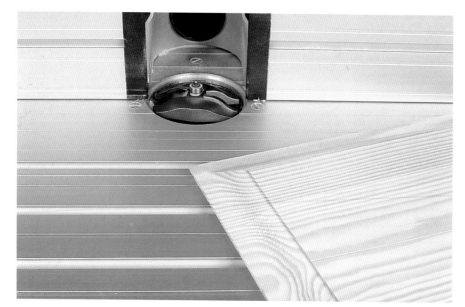

13 Raise the panels, first across the grain and then along the grain to clean up the tear-out. Make several shallow passes.

14 Assemble the doors. Glue the rails to the stiles, but let the panels float in the grooves. Check for square and be sure to rest the door on a flat surface while the glue is drying.

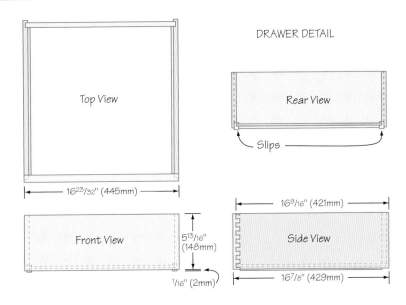

DRAWER DETAIL

Top View

16²³/₃₂" (445mm)

Rear View

Slips

Front View

5¹³/₁₆" (148mm)

1/16" (2mm)

16⁹/₁₆" (421mm)

Side View

16⁷/₈" (429mm)

15 Remove the bulk of the waste from the hinge mortises using a laminate trimmer fitted with a ¹/₂" (13mm) mortising cutter. Square the corners and clean up the mortise using a sharp chisel.

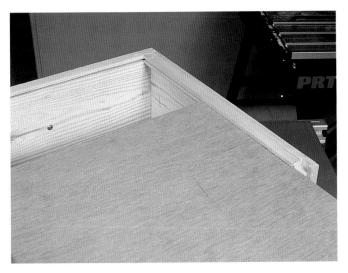

16 Make the drawers with dovetail joints holding the fronts to the sides and dadoes holding the back in place.

17 Make the slips along the edge of a full board by first running the groove into which the bottom fits and then rounding over the edge with a roundover cutter. Then rip the slips from the board so that the groove will coincide with the groove on the rear of the drawer front.

18 Glue the drawer front, sides and back together. Using glue, attach the slips to the bottoms of the sides. Slide the bottom panel into the grooves (use no glue), clamp the drawer, check for square, and secure the bottom with a couple of brads in the bottom of the drawer back.

router trolley

Two things make up the

the constant router user's bane—the power cord and having to park the router between cutting operations. Yes, there are cordless routers, but the demand on the batteries is huge and the additional weight and bulk do nothing to ease the handling. Parking a router is always a problem, especially if it is locked in position with the cutter protruding, as when using cutters with long guides.

This router trolley was designed to solve these problems without creating a whole host

of new ones. This flexible piece has a low center of gravity for stability, a circular design to avoid snagging cords or extraction hoses and compatibility with any router. The design incorporates adequate storage for cutters and tools as well as other router accessories. It also has its own power supply socket to reduce the amount of trailing leads across the workshop at bench height. The most important feature for me is the maneuverability. Its wheels make it easy to move the trolley wherever it's needed, and they can be locked so the trolley will stay put.

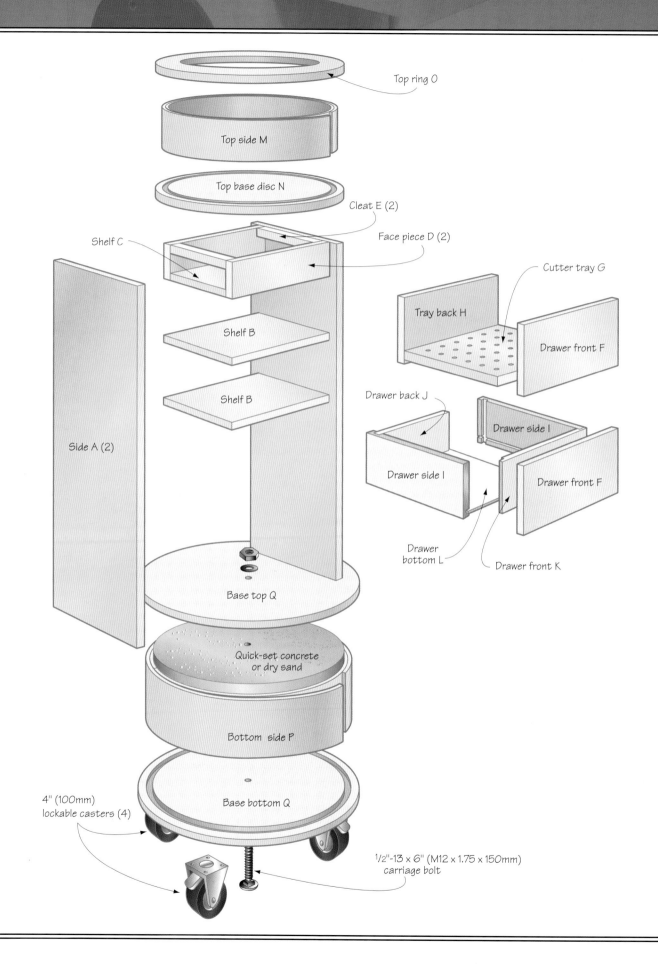

Top ring O

Top side M

Top base disc N

Cleat E (2)

Shelf C

Face piece D (2)

Cutter tray G

Tray back H

Drawer front F

Drawer back J

Drawer side I

Shelf B

Shelf B

Drawer side I

Drawer front F

Side A (2)

Drawer bottom L

Drawer front K

Base top Q

Quick-set concrete or dry sand

Bottom side P

Base bottom Q

4" (100mm) lockable casters (4)

1/2"-13 x 6" (M12 x 1.75 x 150mm) carriage bolt

router trolley — inches (millimeters)

REFERENCE	QUANTITY	PART	STOCK	THICKNESS		WIDTH		LENGTH		COMMENTS
A	2	sides	MDF	3/4	(18)	9⁷/₈	(251)	29¹/₂	(749)	
B	2	shelves	MDF	3/4	(18)	7⁵/₈	(194)	8³/₈	(213)	
C	1	shelf	MDF	3/4	(18)	6¹/₄	(159)	8³/₈	(213)	
D	2	face pieces	MDF	3/4	(18)	3¹/₈	(79)	8³/₈	(213)	
E	2	cleats	softwood	3/4	(18)	3/4	(19)	6	(152)	
F	2	drawer fronts	MDF	3/4	(18)	5³/₄	(146)	8³/₈	(213)	
G	1	cutter tray	MDF	3/4	(18)	6⁷/₈	(175)	8³/₈	(213)	
H	1	tray back	MDF	3/4	(18)	5¹/₈	(130)	8³/₈	(213)	
I	2	drawer sides	softwood	1/2	(12)	4¹/₂	(114)	7⁵/₃₂	(182)	
J	1	drawer back	softwood	1/2	(12)	4¹/₄	(108)	7³/₄	(197)	
K	1	drawer front	softwood	1/2	(12)	4¹/₂	(114)	8³/₈	(213)	
L	1	drawer bottom	plywood	1/4	(6)	7⁵/₃₂	(182)	7³/₄	(197)	
M	2	top sides	flexible MDF	1/4	(6)	3¹/₈	(79)	44³/₈	(1127)	
N	1	top base disc	MDF	3/4	(18)	15³/₄ d	(400)			
O	1	top ring	MDF	3/4	(18)	15³/₄ d	(400)			
P	2	bottom sides	flexible MDF	1/4	(6)	5¹/₂	(140)	59	(1499)	
Q	2	base top and bottom	MDF	3/4	(18)	19³/₄ d	(502)			

hardware & supplies

- plastic sheet
- 1 bag quick-set concrete
- 2 3" (76mm) drawer pulls
- 4 4" (100mm) casters
- 16 3/8"-16 x 1" (M10 x 1.5 x 25mm) carriage bolts
- 16 3/8" (M10) hex nuts
- 16 3/8" (M10) flat washers
- 1 1/2"-13 x 6" (M12 x 1.75 x 150mm) carriage bolt
- 1 1/2" (M12) hex nut
- 1 1/2" (M12) flat washer

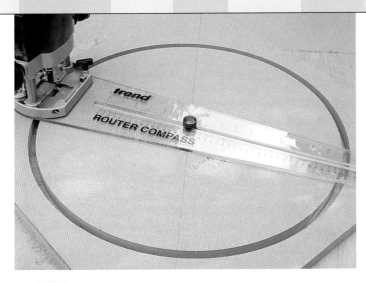

1 To cut out the round parts, place a backer board on the bench with a nonslip router mat underneath it. Secure the blank to the backer board with double-stick tape. Set the router compass to the correct radius and proceed to cut out the circle by making several shallow cuts, each of which should be no more than 3/16" (5mm) deep.

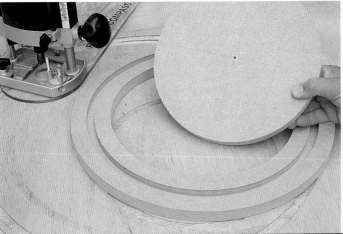

2 To cut the grooves into the discs that require grooves, set the depth stop on the router to 3/8" (10mm) and make the cuts in small increments until you've reached the required depth.

3 Using a trim router fitted with a $\frac{1}{4}$"-radius (6mm) bearing-guided roundover cutter, round over all the edges. Position the wheels so that all the bolts holes are inside the groove. Install the wheels from the other side of the bottom.

4 Insert flexible MDF into the groove and glue it in place. Use the top disc to hold the flexible MDF in place (don't glue the top disc) and apply some clamps to hold the sandwich together until the glue dries.

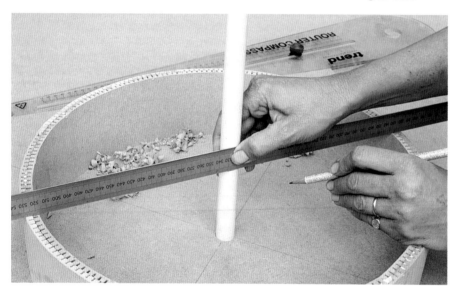

5 To make the mould for the concrete, cut a $\frac{1}{2}$"-wide (13mm) circular groove, $\frac{3}{8}$" (10mm) deep, in a piece of MDF. This groove should be slightly smaller in diameter than the groove cut into the base. Cut some flexible MDF and insert it into the groove. Then insert a $\frac{3}{4}$" (19mm) piece of plastic pipe into the center of the mould.

6 Line the mold with plastic and pour quick-set concrete into it. Use some clamps, if necessary, to hold the mold round. When the concrete has set, remove it from the mold and let it dry for a week.

7 Drill a $\frac{3}{4}$" (19mm) hole in the center of the bottom of the base. Drill some small air holes in the base and line the bottom with plastic. Insert the dry concrete disc upside down, aligning the protruding pipe with the hole in the base.

8 Drill pocket holes in the shelves.

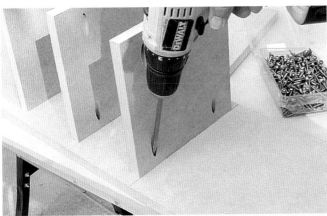

9 Using pocket-hole screws install the shelves on one side of the tower.

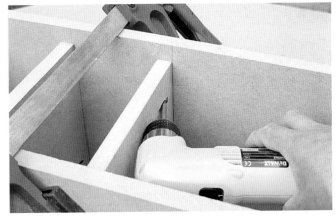

10 Attach the other tower side to the shelves using pocket-hole screws.

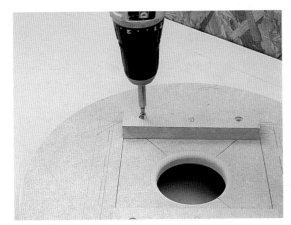

11 Use cleats to situate the router park on the tower. This allows you to remove the top to recover anything that drops inside the void.

12 Round over all the exposed edges of the router park.

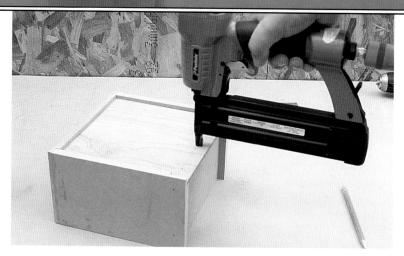

14 Cut out the drawer parts and assemble the drawer, securing the bottom using brads.

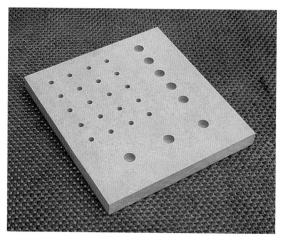

15 The base of the cutter tray is drilled with $1/4$" (6mm) and $1/2$" (13mm) holes for various sizes of router cutters.

13 Attach the tower to the bottom using glue and screws. Then run a bolt up through the pipe and through the tower base. Secure the whole base assembly with a washer and nut. Attach the router park to the tower using screws and no glue.

16 Attach the front to the cutter tray using glue and pocket-screws.

17 Attach a power switch and box to the side of the tower.

using the router trolley

The tool drawer will hold extra collets, wrenches, small clamps and whatever else you need to operate your router.

The cutter tray is easily accessible and keeps cutters within easy reach.

The router park is perfect for holding your router when it's not in use and is large enough to take the largest of routers with a long cutter installed.

When not in use, the trolley can be easily tucked away in a corner.

You can hang any fences or other accessories on the side of the trolley's tower.

computer
station

If you had told me a

while back that my life would revolve around computer use, I probably would have laughed at you. While all around me were diving headlong into mega this and pixel that, I was struggling to program the VCR.

A few years down the road and here I am bashing keys and looking at a computer screen for a big chunk of the day. Okay, I had to sit here to write this book, but I spend a lot of time designing and working out jobs, using CAD programs, "talking" to fellow woodworkers around the world and doing general research.

The thought of running a computer in the workshop was not entertained with any enthusiasm due to expense and problems with dust. As time has passed and my reliance on the electronic abacus has grown, the expense and problems have diminished.

For me part of the solution is to use a desktop PC with a few modifications: a wireless

optical mouse and keyboard. The CPU and monitor can be housed in a cabinet with a clear acrylic panel allowing the screen to be viewed. The mouse and keyboard can be kept in a drawer.

This was the initial plan. Then an American friend mentioned that his keyboard could be put in the dishwasher! It is called "the indestructible keyboard." Although it needs to be hardwired it can be left out amidst the sawdust, coffee cups and any other hazards.

So, the workshop system will be made up of an old(ish) CPU and a 15" monitor housed inside a fixed cabinet that has a fan-driven air intake to pull in dust-free air from outside the workshop. There is also room inside the cabinet for a printer. The keyboard and mouse are housed on a rigid shelf. This can be a drawer if you want to use and protect a conventional keyboard. My system is linked to the computer in the house via an Ethernet card and a crossover cable.

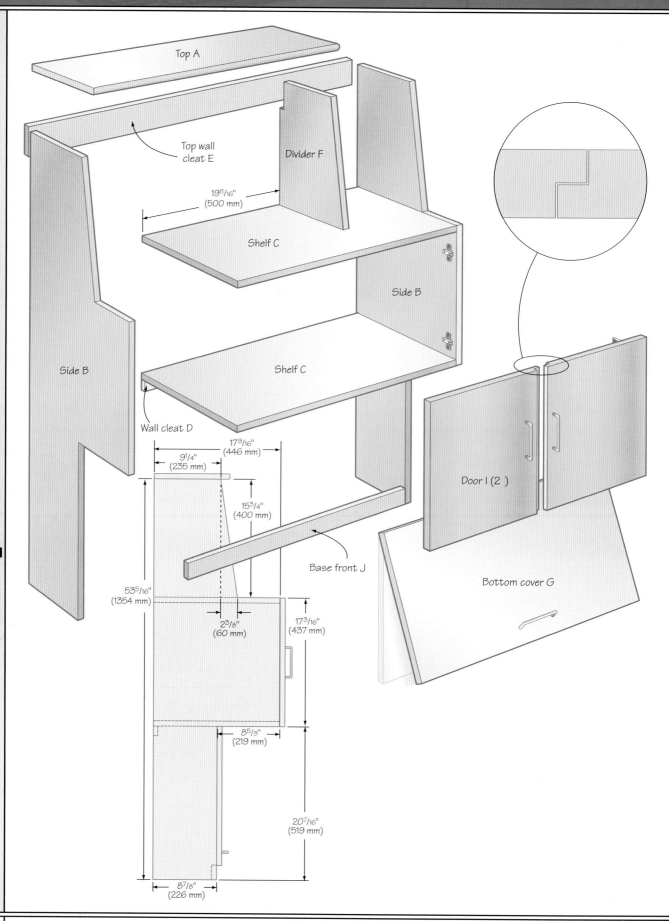

Top A

Top wall cleat E

Divider F

19¹¹/₁₆" (500 mm)

Shelf C

Side B

Side B

Shelf C

Wall cleat D

17⁹/₁₆" (446 mm)

9¹/₄" (235 mm)

15³/₄" (400 mm)

Base front J

Door I (2)

Bottom cover G

53⁵/₁₆" (1354 mm)

2³/₈" (60 mm)

17³/₁₆" (437 mm)

8⁵/₈" (219 mm)

20⁷/₁₆" (519 mm)

8⁷/₈" (226 mm)

computer station   inches (millimeters)

REFERENCE	QUANTITY	PART	STOCK	THICKNESS		WIDTH		LENGTH		COMMENTS
A	1	top	MDF	3/4	(18)	10	(254)	33^{15}/$_{16}$	(862)	
B	2	sides	MDF	3/4	(18)	17^9/$_{16}$	(446)	53^5/$_{16}$	(1354)	
C	2	shelves	MDF	3/4	(18)	17^9/$_{16}$	(446)	31^7/$_{16}$	(799)	
D	1	wall cleat	MDF	3/4	(18)	1^1/$_2$	(38)	31^7/$_{16}$	(799)	
E	1	top wall cleat	MDF	3/4	(18)	4	(102)	31^7/$_{16}$	(799)	
F	1	divider	MDF	3/4	(18)	11^5/$_8$	(295)	15	(381)	
G	1	bottom cover	MDF	3/4	(18)	18^7/$_{16}$	(468)	32^{15}/$_{16}$	(837)	
H	1	inner cover panel	MDF	1/2	(12)	17^5/$_8$	(448)	31^3/$_8$	(797)	installed on inside of bottom cover
I	2	doors	MDF	3/4	(18)	16^3/$_4$	(425)	17^3/$_{16}$	(437)	
J	1	base front	MDF	3/4	(18)	2	(51)	31^7/$_{16}$	(799)	

hardware & supplies

4   170° overlay self-closing Eurohinges with mounting plates

3   4" (100mm) handles

    1/4" (6mm)-thick acrylic panel cut to fit computer opening

4   1/2" (13mm) x 1/2" (13mm) cleats for mounting acrylic panel

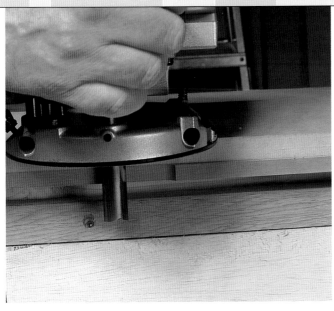

1 Cut out the parts according to the cutting list. Then round over the edges to smooth them.

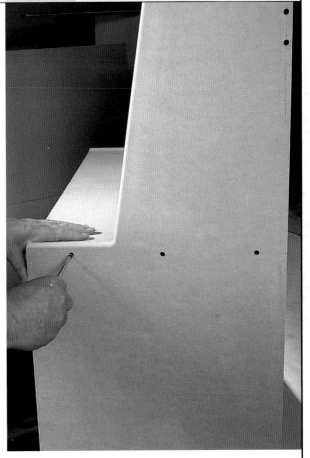

2 Using biscuits, glue and screws, assemble the cabinet.

3 Fit the vertical divider between the monitor enclosure and the storage compartment. Install the cleats on the left side and vertical divider that hold the acrylic panel in place.

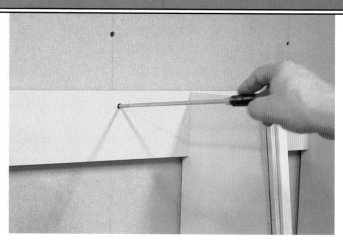

4 Affix the carcass to the wall through the cross brace.

5 Install the top of the station. Then install the top and bottom cleats that hold the acrylic panel. After the monitor is in place, install the acrylic panel using four cleats screwed to the side, vertical divider, top and shelf. The keyboard will sit in front of the acrylic panel.

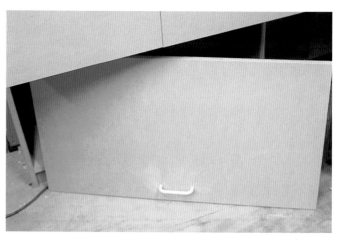

6 Laminate a piece of 1/2" (12mm) MDF to the inside of the lower cover to creat a lip around the edges that will hold the cover in place. This way, when the CPU needs to be accessed the cover can be completely removed.

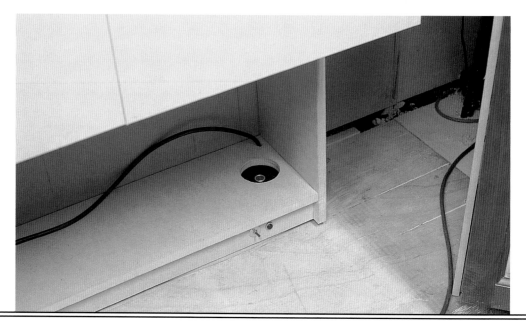

7 For the airflow and cable access use a plastic pipe that is large enough to allow the plugs to pass through easily.

8 Cut out the doors and cut a rabbet on one long edge of each door. These rabbets are cut opposite of each other. See the illustration for details. Then drill the holes for the Eurohinges.

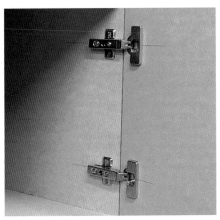

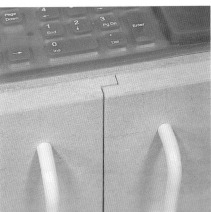

9 Set the mounting plates on the carcass at the same spacing as the holes on the doors. For exact positioning of the mounting plates, refer to the manufacturer's instructions.

10 The rabbets on the doors will help keep the dust out.

11 Plug the carcass holes and sand the plugs flush to the sides of the cabinet.

12 Make connections via the pipe.

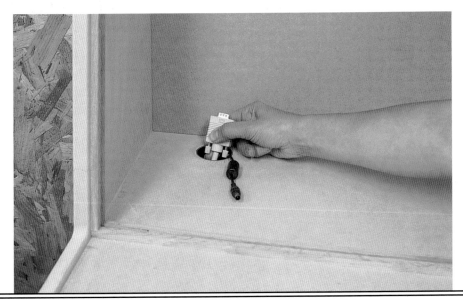

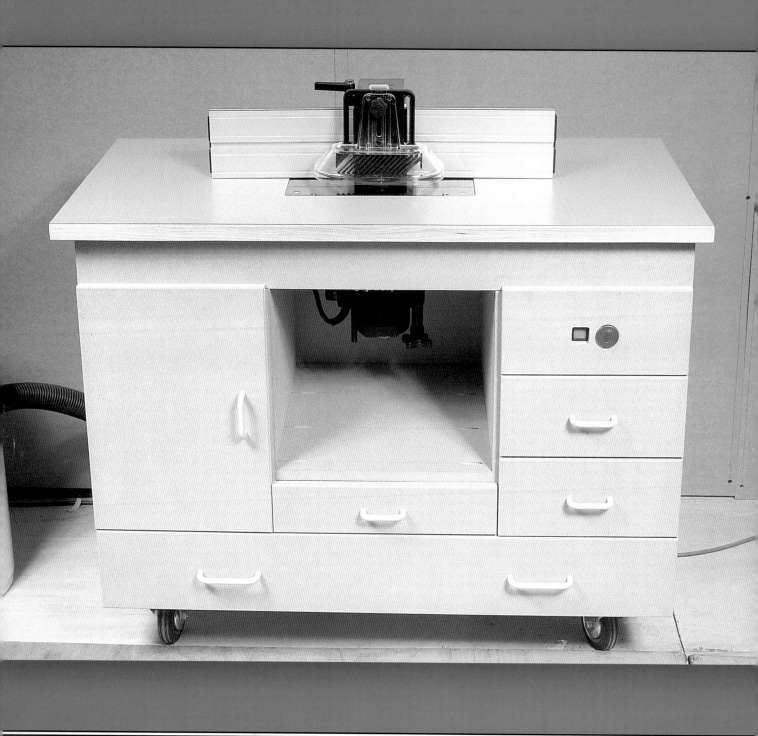

router table

My router
table is of a

conventional design with plenty of
storage and a practical size.

My criteria are fairly open. I
want to adopt a standard height for
units wherever possible. The router
table has to be mobile within the workshop and
most importantly, it needs to be capable of handling and containing much of the dust that a
router used in a confined space will make.

A mobile unit such as this should carry all
the paraphernalia that goes with routing. Taking
this into account, a cabinet-style base with storage and a sealed router compart-
ment are the dictates that define
this design.

Solidity with a mobile unit is
best accomplished by giving it mass;
you can do this easily by building it
from substantial materials. Don't forget, once completed it will roll over
the floor with ease, so weight is not an issue.
The cabinet, dividers, drawer fronts and door
should all be cut from ¾"-thick (18mm) MDF.

Consider the wheels. The larger the wheel
the less likely it will be to stall on a small piece
of debris on the floor. The wheels used here are
4" (100mm) in diameter.

router table construction notes

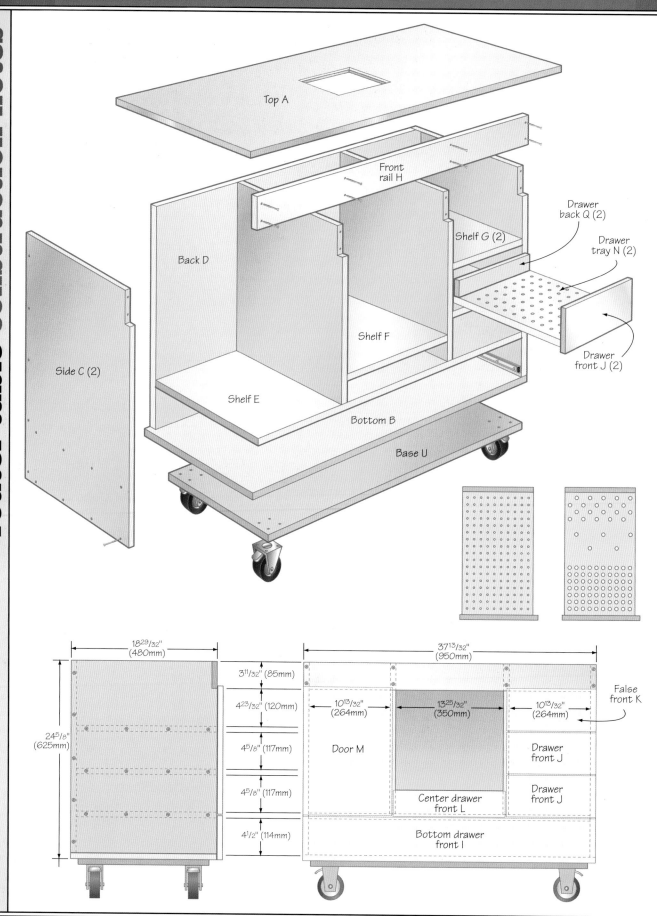

Top A

Front rail H

Back D

Shelf G (2)

Drawer back Q (2)

Drawer tray N (2)

Shelf F

Side C (2)

Drawer front J (2)

Shelf E

Bottom B

Base U

18²⁹/₃₂"
(480mm)

37¹³/₃₂"
(950mm)

3¹¹/₃₂" (85mm)

4²³/₃₂" (120mm)

10¹³/₃₂"
(264mm)

13²⁵/₃₂"
(350mm)

10¹³/₃₂"
(264mm)

False front K

24⁵/₈"
(625mm)

4⁵/₈" (117mm)

Door M

Drawer front J

4⁵/₈" (117mm)

Drawer front J

4¹/₂" (114mm)

Center drawer front L

Bottom drawer front I

router table inches (millimeters)

REFERENCE	QUANTITY	PART	STOCK	THICKNESS		WIDTH		LENGTH		COMMENTS
A	1	top	MDF	1	(25)	$20^7/8$	(530)	$39^1/2$	(1003)	
B	1	bottom	MDF	$3/4$	(18)	$18^{29}/32$	(480)	$37^7/16$	(950)	
C	2	sides	MDF	$3/4$	(18)	$18^{29}/32$	(480)	$23^7/8$	(606)	
D	1	back	MDF	$3/4$	(18)	$23^7/8$	(606)	$35^{15}/16$	(913)	
E	1	shelf	MDF	$3/4$	(18)	$18^1/8$	(460)	$35^{15}/16$	(913)	
F	1	shelf	MDF	$3/4$	(18)	$13^3/4$	(349)	$18^1/8$	(460)	
G	2	shelves	MDF	$3/4$	(18)	$10^3/8$	(264)	$18^1/8$	(460)	
H	1	front rail	MDF	$3/4$	(18)	$3^{11}/32$	(85)	$37^{15}/32$	(950)	
I	1	bottom drawer front	MDF	$3/4$	(18)	$5^1/2$	(140)	$37^{15}/32$	(950)	
J	2	drawer fronts	MDF	$3/4$	(18)	$5^1/8$	(130)	$11^3/8$	(289)	
K	1	false front	MDF	$3/4$	(18)	$5^1/4$	(133)	$11^3/8$	(289)	
L	1	center drawer front	MDF	$3/4$	(18)	$3^3/8$	(86)	$14^1/4$	(362)	
M	1	door	MDF	$3/4$	(18)	$11^3/8$	(289)	$15^7/8$ h	(403)	
N	2	drawer trays	MDF	$3/4$	(18)	$10^3/8$	(264)	$18^1/8$	(460)	
O	1	center drawer tray	MDF	$3/4$	(18)	$13^3/4$	(349)	$18^1/8$	(460)	
P	1	bottom drawer tray	MDF	$3/4$	(18)	$18^1/8$	(460)	$35^{15}/16$	(913)	
Q	2	drawer backs	MDF	$3/4$	(18)	$4^5/8$	(117)	$10^3/8$	(264)	
R	1	center drawer back	MDF	$3/4$	(18)	$2^3/8$	(60)	$13^3/4$	(349)	
S	1	bottom drawer back	MDF	$3/4$	(18)	$4^1/2$	(114)	$35^{15}/16$	(913)	
T	1	base	MDF	$3/4$	(18)	17	(432)	$35^1/2$	(902)	

hardware & supplies

- 2   170° full-overlay self-closing Eurohinge with mounting plates
- 4   4"(100mm)-diameter lockable casters
- 16 $3/8$"-16 x 1"(M10 x 1.5 x 25mm) carriage bolts
- 16 $3/8$" (M10) hex nuts
- 16 $3/8$" (M10) flat washers
- 6   4" (100mm) handles
- 1   set 18" (500mm) drawer slides
- 1   22" (559mm) x 41" (1041mm) sheet of laminate
- $1/2$" (13mm) x $3/4$" (18mm) x 130" (330cm) hardwood edging

1 Cut out all of the parts according to the cutting list. The use of $3/4$"-thick (18mm) material for the drawers is not usual, but in this case the added weight will aid stability. To hold together the entire carcass and the drawer assemblies use pocket holes and pocket-hole screws.

2 Use a batten to align the intermediate pieces. This ensures that the openings will be square.

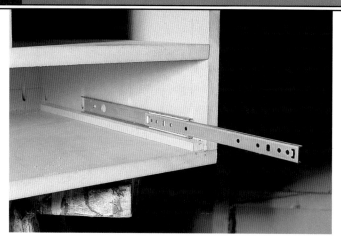

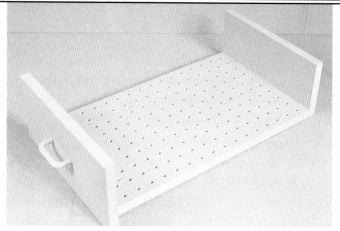

3 Use a spacer to fit the drawer runners. Keeping the runners up from the bottom makes it easier to install the hardware.

4 Drill lots of holes to give you plenty of room for all your cutters. The spacing is purely a matter of preference. In the tray with $1/4$"(6mm) diameter holes, I use a 1" (25mm) grid. Holes can be left empty if the cutters crowd each other. The tray with $1/2$"(13mm) diameter holes has holes spaced to take large cutters as well as a block of holes on a 1" (25mm) grid.

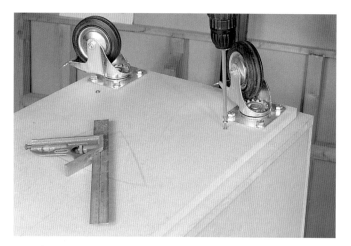

5 Install the casters on the base using bolts, washers and nuts. Then attach the base to the bottom of the table.

6 Attach the front rail using glue and pocket-hole screws.

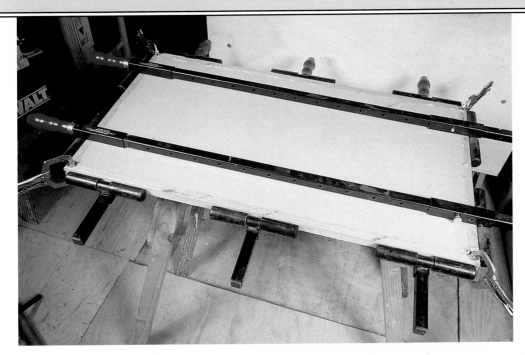

7 Use biscuits and glue to attach hardwood edges to the top.

8 Trim the hardwood edges flush to the top and bottom surfaces of the top.

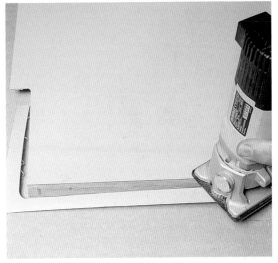

9 Apply the laminate to the top using contact cement. Use a trim router fitted with a beveled cutter to trim the laminate flush to the edges of the top.

10 Mark the location of the aperture for the router plate. Tape the guides in place using double-stick tape, then rout the template aperture.

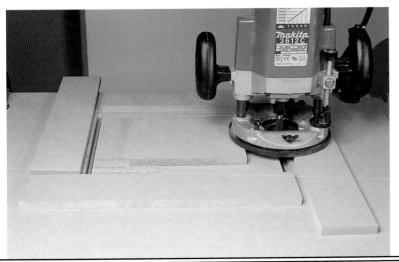

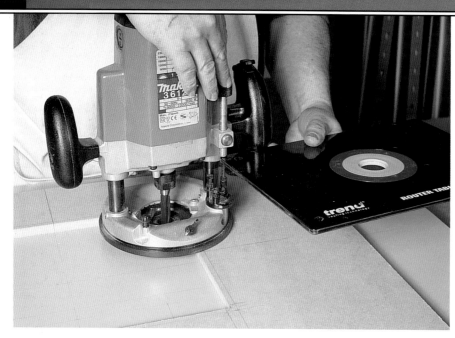

11 Set the depth of the rabbet using the router plate as a gauge.

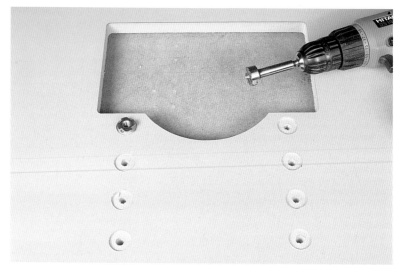

12 Cut the arc in the cutout. The masking tape around the router base will prevent it from scratching the laminate while you make the cut through the top in ¼" (6mm) increments.

14 On the top surface, seat the T-nuts in the cut-out using nuts, washers and a bolt. This method is much less traumatic for the top than hammering them home.

13 On the underside of the top, drill the T-nut recesses.

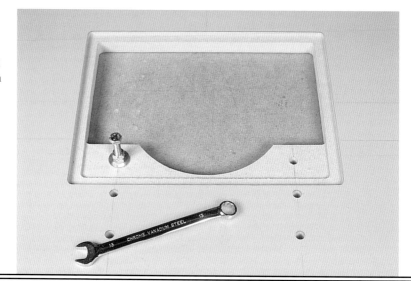

setup of a purchased fence and router mounting insert

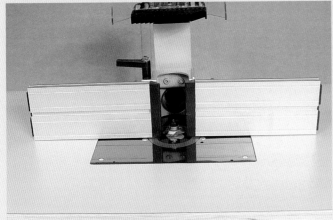

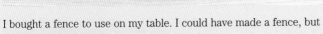

I bought a fence to use on my table. I could have made a fence, but this was much easier!

The router table insert comes predrilled for a starter pin.

Mount the router on the inset plate. Use threaded bolts to hold the plate tight at the front of the plate.

Use the leveling kit threaded inserts to secure the rear of the plate.

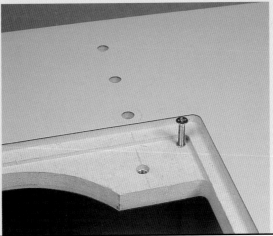

suppliers

ADAMS & KENNEDY — THE WOOD SOURCE
6178 Mitch Owen Rd.
P.O. Box 700
Manotick, ON
Canada K4M 1A6
613-822-6800
www.wood-source.com
Wood supply

AXMINSTER POWER TOOL CENTRE LTD.
Unit 10 Weycroft Avenue
Axminster
Devon
EX13 5PH United Kingdom
0800 371822
www.axminster.co.uk
Tools, hardware, books, finishing supplies, veneers and turning blanks

ADJUSTABLE CLAMP COMPANY
404 N. Armour St.
Chicago, IL 60622
312-666-0640
www.adjustableclamp.com
Clamps and woodworking tools

B&Q
Portswood House
1 Hampshire Corporate Park
Chandlers Ford
Eastleigh
Hampshire, England SO53 3YX
0845 609 6688
www.diy.com
Woodworking tools, supplies and hardware

CONSTANTINE'S WOOD CENTER OF FLORIDA
1040 E. Oakland Park Blvd.
Fort Lauderdale, FL 33334
800-443-9667
www.constantines.com
Tools, woods, veneers, hardware

FRANK PAXTON LUMBER COMPANY
5701 W. Sixty-sixth St.
Chicago, IL 60638
800-323-2203
www.paxtonwood.com
Wood, hardware, tools, books

THE HOME DEPOT
2455 Paces Ferry Rd.
Atlanta, GA 30339
800-553-3199 (U.S.)
800-628-0525 (Canada)
www.homedepot.com
Woodworking tools, supplies and hardware

LEE VALLEY TOOLS LTD.
P.O. Box 1780
Ogdensburg, NY 13669-6780
800-871-8158 (U.S.)
800-267-8767 (Canada)
www.leevalley.com
Woodworking tools and hardware

LOWE'S
P.O. Box 1111
North Wilkesboro, NC 28656
800-445-6937
www.lowes.com
Woodworking tools, supplies and hardware

ROCKLER WOODWORKING AND HARDWARE
4365 Willow Dr.
Medina, MN 55340
800-279-4441
www.rockler.com
Woodworking tools, hardware and books

TOOL TREND LTD.
140 Snow Blvd.
Thornhill, ON
Canada L4K 4L1
416-663-8665
Woodworking tools and hardware

TREND MACHINERY & CUTTING TOOLS LTD.
Odhams Trading Estate
St. Albans Rd.
Watford
Hertfordshire, U.K.
WD24 7TR
01923 224657
www.trendmachinery.co.uk
Woodworking tools and hardware

VAUGHAN & BUSHNELL MFG. CO.
11414 Maple Ave.
Hebron, IL 60034
815-648-2446
www.vaughanmfg.com
Hammers and other tools

WOODCRAFT SUPPLY CORP.
1177 Rosemar Rd.
P.O. Box 1686
Parkersburg, WV 26102
800-535-4482
www.woodcraft.com
Woodworking hardware

WOODWORKER'S HARDWARE
P.O. Box 180
Sauk Rapids, MN 56379-0180
800-383-0130
www.wwhardware.com
Woodworking hardware

WOODWORKER'S SUPPLY
1108 N. Glenn Rd.
Casper, WY 82601
800-645-9292
http://woodworker.com
Woodworking tools and accessories, finishing supplies, books and plans

C

Cabinets
  computer station, 112–117
  drill press, 36–45
  free-standing, 96–103
  hanging of, 35
  router cutters storage, 26–35
  wall-hanging, 62–69
Chemical safety notice, 2
Chest, small items, 18–25
Chisel rack, 7–11
  assembly, 11
  construction notes, 10
  overview, 9
  supplies, 10
Clamp stand, 78–83
  assembly, 81–83
  construction notes, 80
  hardware and supplies, 81
  overview, 79
Computer station, 112–117
  assembly, 115–117
  construction notes, 114
  hardware and supplies, 115
  overview, 113

D

Doors
  computer station, 114, 117
  drill press cabinet, 38, 41–42,
    45
  free-standing cabinet, 98,
    102–103
  mobile saw table stand, 89
  router cutters storage cabi-
    net, 28, 30–32
  wall-hanging cabinet, 64,
    66–69
Dovetails, 31
Downdraft table, 70–77
  assembly, 73–77
  construction notes, 72
  hardware and supplies, 73
  overview, 71
  vacuum specifications, 75
Drawers
  free-standing cabinet, 103
  router table, 122
  router trolley, 110–111
  small items chest, 20–25

Drill press cabinet, 36–45
  assembly, 39–45
  construction notes, 38
  hardware and supplies, 39
  overview, 37
Dust extractor specifications,
  downdraft table, 75

F

Free-standing cabinet, 96–103
  assembly, 99–103
  construction notes, 98
  overview, 97
  supplies, 99

G

Glass shelving, safety notice, 2

H

Hole-cutting
  chisel rack, 11
  downdraft table, 72, 75, 76
  router cutters storage cabi-
    net, 32–33
  router table, 122
  router trolley, 110
  tool tote, 52

M

Metric conversion chart, 2
Mobile saw table stand, 84–89
  assembly, 87–89
  construction notes, 86
  hardware and supplies, 87
  overview, 85

O

Outfeed table, 90–95
  assembly, 93–95
  construction notes, 92
  hardware and supplies, 93
  overview, 91

P

Power equipment safety notice,
  2

R

Router cutters storage cabinet,
  26–35

assembly, 29–35
construction notes, 28
dovetails, 31
hanging the cabinet, 35
hardware and supplies, 29
overview, 27
Router table, 118–125
  assembly, 121–124
  construction notes, 120
  hardware and supplies, 121
  overview, 119
  setup of fence and mounting
    insert, 125
Router trolley, 104–111
  assembly, 107–111
  construction notes, 106
  hardware and supplies, 107
  overview, 105

S

Safety notice, 2
Sandpaper press, 12–17
  assembly, 15–17
  construction notes, 14
  hardware and supplies, 15
  overview, 13
Saw table stand, 84–89
Small items chest, 18–25
  assembly, 21–25
  construction notes, 20
  hardware and supplies, 21
  overview, 19
Small offcuts storage trolley,
  54–61
  assembly, 57–61
  construction notes, 56
  hardware and supplies, 57
  overview, 55
Stool, 46–49, 53
  assembly, 49, 53
  construction notes, 48
  overview, 47
  supplies, 49
Storage trolley for small offcuts,
  54–61
Suppliers, 126

T

Tables
  downdraft table, 70–77
  mobile saw table stand, 84–89
  outfeed table, 90–95
  router table, 118–125
Tool tote, 46–53
  assembly, 49–53
  construction notes, 48
  overview, 47
  supplies, 49
Trolleys
  router trolley, 104–111
  small offcuts storage trolley,
    54–61

V

Vacuum specifications, downdraft table, 75

W

Wall-hanging cabinet, 62–69
  assembly, 65–69
  construction notes, 64
  hardware and supplies, 65
  overview, 63
Wheels for trolley, 59–61

More great titles from Popular Woodworking!

Glen Huey's Illustrated Guide to Building Period Furniture

By Glen Huey
Woodworkers will learn to build their own high-end period furniture with clear, concise instructions, step-by-step photos and a bonus DVD ROM of real-time demonstrations and printable plans.

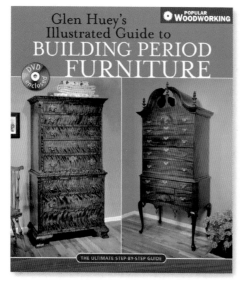

ISBN 13: 978-1-55870-770-2
ISBN 10: 1-55870-770-0, pb, 128 p, #70722

The Complete Cabinetmaker's Reference

By Jeffrey Piontkowski
This indispensable resource for cabinetmakers includes cutting and assembly instructions, along with lists of types and quantities of materials needed for all standard-sized cabinets. You'll also learn how to adapt the projects to build custom-sized pieces.

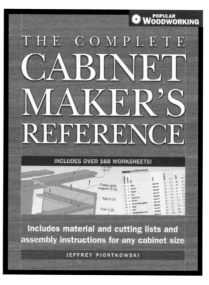

ISBN 13: 978-1-55870-757-3
ISBN 10: 1-55870-757-3, pb, 128 p, #70710

Popular Woodworking Pocket Shop Reference

By Tom Begnal
Woodworkers will find concise and accurate information about a broad range of woodworking topics, covering everything from furniture design and materials to adhesives, tools, safety and more. Lay flat binding and handy pocket size make this easy-to-reference guide the perfect resource for any woodshop.

ISBN 13: 978-1-55870-782-5
ISBN 10: 1-55870-782-4
hc w/ concealed wire-o
240 p., # Z0227

Popular Woodworking Practical Shop Math

By Tom Begnal
Portable and easy-to-use, this handy guide makes the perfect comprehensive "cheat sheet" to woodworking math. It explains math formulas and conversions in simple layman's terms, and includes sections on working with fractions and decimals, dimensioned drawings and more.

ISBN 13: 978-1-55870-783-2
ISBN 10: 1-55870-783-2
hc w/ concealed wire-o
240 p., # Z0226

These and other great woodworking books are available at your local bookstore, woodworking stores, or from online suppliers.

www.popularwoodworking.com